ROCKIN' DOWN THE HIGHWAY TO HELL

Discovering the Hidden Satanic Power Behind Today's Music

Michael Bruce Plont

Traverse City, Michigan

ROCKIN' DOWN THE HIGHWAY TO HELL
Discovering the Hidden Satanic Power Behind Today's Music
by Michael Bruce Plont

Published by:

BookMarketingSolutions LLC

10300 E. Leelanau Ct.
Traverse City MI 49684 U.S.A.
orders@BookMarketingSolutions.com
www.BookMarketingSolutions.com

All rights reserved. No part of this book may be reproduced or transmitted in any form or by any means, electronic or mechanical, including photocopying, recording or by any information storage and retrieval system, without written permission from the publisher, except for the inclusion of brief quotations in a review.

Copyright © 2005 by Michael Bruce Plont

Plont, Michael Bruce.
Rockin' down the highway to hell : discovering the hidden Satanic
power behind today's music / Michael Bruce Plont. --
Traverse City,
MI : Book Marketing Solutions, 2005.
p. ; cm.
Includes bibliographical references and index.
ISBN: 0-9741345-1-1
1. Rock music--Religious aspects--Christianity. 2. Rock music--
Psychological aspects. I. Title.
ML3534 .P56 2005
781.66--dc22 0506

This book is dedicated to Malachi James:
I earnestly wait for the day that my tears will be wiped away, and my son will be in my arms, in heaven.

CONTENTS

Chapter 1	Drawn Away	12
Chapter 2	Those Evil Eyes	14
Chapter 3	Biblical History	16
Chapter 4	Aleister Crowley	22
Chapter 5	Hooked	26
Chapter 6	Kenneth Anger	28
Chapter 7	Dominoes	33
Chapter 8	Aldous Huxley	37
Chapter 9	Inoculated	40
Chapter 10	Timothy Leary	42
Chapter 11	Twisted	48
Chapter 12	In the Net	51
Chapter 13	The Cough	54
Chapter 14	Hezekiah Ben Aaron	57
Chapter 15	The Field	59
Chapter 16	Anton LaVey	61
Chapter 17	Stunted Growth	64
Chapter 18	Jeff Fenholt	67
Chapter 19	Vile Worship	69
Chapter 20	The Power of Music	72

CONTENTS

Chapter 21	The Sidewalk	91
Chapter 22	Covered Up	93
Chapter 23	The Vow	96
Chapter 24	Stoned	98
Chapter 25	In Chains	100
Chapter 26	The Jungle	103
Chapter 27	Hero	107
Chapter 28	Boomerang	109
Chapter 29	The Cigar	111
Chapter 30	The Last Song	113
Chapter 31	The New Song	115
Chapter 32	Christian Music?	118
Chapter 33	Don't Kid Yourself	122
Chapter 34	Guilty	142
Index		149
About the Author		153

ACKNOWLEDGMENTS

A few words of thanks to:

Pastor Michael Wermuth: For being the Paul in my life and the first editor in this book.

Pastor Daniel Davis and MT ZION FWC: for being supportive and Christ Like, there is no place I'd rather serve.

Tom White and BMS Staff: thank you beyond measure for taking a chance on me.

Sylvia Rogers: for being bold enough to confront me, and loving enough to walk beside me.

Rev. Dan McCabe: for inspiring me to write this book.

My Father, Mother, and Sister: Thank you for allowing me to tell my story, and I thank God we are all saved.

Micah: There is not a father who is more proud or fortunate than I.

My wife Kelli: Thank you for loving a man with a past, you're my best friend.

And to Jesus: no words could explain my appreciation for saving and changing me, may this book glorify your name.

INTRODUCTION

I would be a fool to say that I wrote this book on my own. It was written in simple obedience to my Father, God. I am also not stating that every word of it was inspired by God the way that the Bible was. It is simply the story of a man who has been given a calling to complete.

I considered myself a good person. I had no reason to doubt that because of my good deeds, I was headed for heaven. But, I can clearly state to you today, I would have burned in hell. That in itself is humbling beyond measure. The day I accepted Jesus Christ into my heart and into my life, I became a new man. He opened my eyes to the truth.

This is the story of my life. It tells how I became addicted, who was providing the bait, and how I was ultimately freed from it. This book will take you back in time, even years before I was born. It has to. It has to establish a foundation to show you how the music industry has lowered itself to the despicable point where it is today.

I was bound by popular music for years on end, and the not-so-funny part was, I didn't know it. I had no true explanation for my desires, the thought patterns I formed, or for the choices I was making; I was merely a puppet in a much bigger game. But make no mistake about it, I chose to listen to that music.

My prayer is that this book will be an eye-opener to the truth behind the music. The devil has sought your soul from birth and is wrestling for it today. I want to remind you that he is the most subtle beast of the field. He does not come knocking loudly on your front door. He simply slithers in through the back; he is slow, he is deliberate, he is cunning. He has one thought and one purpose: to draw you away from the One who can fill that large void in your life. He wants your soul and will do anything he can to take hold of it, even serenade you for it.

When you come to the chapters that deal directly with my life, you will see that they start with a song.

Those songs were my favorites during particular periods of time. The chapters are also followed by a related piece of scripture.

This book includes many names of friends or acquaintances with whom I interacted. Their names have been changed to protect the innocent, or in many cases, the guilty. It is my sincere hope that those people already have or will also find the one true God, Jesus Christ. As some of you know, before receiving Christ into my life, I was involved in two marriages. No part of this book involves stories or situations which include either lady. It is my heartfelt prayer that they will know and serve Jesus, and be blessed beyond measure in all that they do.

Well, as they say, let's get on with the show, and may God bless you for reading my story.

Chapter 1

DRAWN AWAY

> "I wanna f--- U so bad it hurts, it hurts, it hurts,
> I wanna, I wanna, I wanna, I wanna, I wanna,
> I wanna f--- U.
> Yeah, I wanna, I wanna, I wanna wanna I wanna f--- U.
> Look here Marsha, I'm not sayin' this just 2 be nasty,
> I sincerely wanna f--- the taste out of your mouth.
> Can U relate?"
> "Let's Pretend We're Married" by Prince
> (www.lyricsondemand.com)

"Let's Pretend We're Married" played on the headphones as I listened in amazement. I had seen *Penthouse* magazine at our neighborhood treehouse. I had stolen racy magazines from my uncle. I had heard the neighborhood boys cuss and tell stories, but nothing like this.

I was 14 and on the way to Mackinac Island with my eighth grade class. My friends were going way beyond the kissing stage with their girlfriends. My soon-to-be crush, Veronica, was drinking her vodka-laced soda pop and my girlfriend Shanna was wanting to French kiss. This was enough to shock me already, but then Billy Doby let me hear his Prince tape. Billy was that kid in your school who was always about three years ahead of everyone else on the sin chart. He was a wild man way beyond me, but I had to be his friend because, well . . . I wanted to date his sister.

"Listen to this," Billy said, chuckling. I put on the headphones and listened. As the words chimed through my ears, a new wall of innocence was torn down. "Whoa, play it again," I said. He did. Over and over and over.

That song began to mold my mind-set into one that would control me for the next 15 years. I had never even closed-mouthed kissed a girl yet (and wouldn't for three more years), but my way of thinking was changing. Women were not someone to whom you show affection, but rather the contrary. They were "tools to complete a job." I was no exception to the hand roaming, but I refused to kiss out of fear of being criticized for bad technique. Isn't it amazing that I refused to do what is probably one of the most intimate, God-ordained love languages one person can show to another? Yet I was more then willing to take part in the animalistic groping.

Eighth grade was a year in development for many of us. The year was 1983, and groups like AC/DC, the Rolling Stones, and REO Speedwagon were on top of the music world. Boy/girl parties were the "in" thing, along with experimenting with cigarettes and alcohol. There was already a list of girls in our class that would go "topless" (or bottomless for that matter). At the young age of 14, we were still babes, yet on the brink of becoming brainwashed adults.

by AC/DC, like "You Shook Me All Night Long," "Love at First Feel," and "Giving the Dog a Bone." Or sexual songs like "Urgent" by the band Foreigner, and "Emotional Rescue" by the Rolling Stones. Don't forget the above mentioned Prince song, and a host of others. We were not participating in love acts, in fact quite the contrary. We were participating in acts that I believed are best described by my college professor, the Reverend Vernell Ingle, as things that "any two dogs can do in the front yard."

"But each one is tempted when he is drawn away by his own desires and enticed."
James 1:14

"The soul of the wicked desires evil . . ."
Proverbs 21:10

Chapter 2

THOSE EVIL EYES

As I would lay myself down to sleep at night, I would see them. I imagine I was around four or five years old when they started, although I can't remember a time when I didn't see them. Every night when I put my head down to rest, I would see these little green, red and yellow dots. They would act much like a kaleidoscope, spinning in circles. Then they would turn into eyes.

They were evil, and they would flash from one set to another approximately every second. Each step I took into the realm of popular music brought on more and more eyes. It went from a nighttime thing to seeing them every time I closed my eyes. It began to haunt me, but after a while I learned to live with it.

I first became interested in and influenced by popular music at a young age. It was on the radio in my home and in my friends' homes. I remember learning to dance to it at about 12 years of age and then attending high school dances from age 12 to 19. As this book will show, in junior high it became my passion and desire to be in a rock band. I pursued it until the time of salvation, and all along I was still seeing the "eyes."

I would be in church, praising the Lord with my eyes closed, and I would see the eyes flashing. It bothered me, but I was putting up with it. It was not until I viewed the ministry video *Hells Bells* that I realized I was addicted to the music and needed to be delivered. I was headed out to do street ministry and I asked the prayer team to pray for my deliverance. I was slain in the Spirit of God for several minutes, but then arose. When I got up, God told me, "YOU WILL NO LONGER SEE THE EYES."

That is how I got to this point. This book will present my story. It would become monotonous to tell you throughout this book each time I saw the eyes. I saw them until I was prayed for. Remember, without the mercy of God, I could have died of my sins at any time, and I would have spent eternity in hell. I won't now, and you do not have to either. The choice is yours, and we will talk about that at the end of this book.

One very important thing to remember is to not do yourself a disservice. You may never have seen the eyes, or even anything close to it, but if you have ever listened to popular music, it has affected you. Read on, my brother or sister, and keep an open mind.

Chapter 3

BIBLICAL HISTORY

I want to start this book by telling you a little bit about how my ministry was started. Before I came to know Jesus, as I said in the previous chapter, I was very determined to make it in the world of rock and roll. I had been pursuing my dream of being the lead singer in a rock band for 14 years. Obviously, that was not God's plan.

As this book will reveal, I hit absolute rock bottom before meeting my Savior. I was going through my second divorce and was flirting with the notion of suicide when I was invited to church. In my desperate search of something, I went to Mt. Zion Family Worship Center in Traverse City, Michigan. That is where I met my best friend, and the Savior of the world, Jesus Christ.

A short time after salvation, I was riding to church with my godmother, Sylvia Rogers. We were listening to heavy metal music (not her choice) and she asked me, "Does this music make you feel good, honey?" I wanted with all my pride to answer, "Yes," but I couldn't. It would have been a lie. Instead, I softly answered, "No." She then changed the radio to a Christian station. I could not stand this particular type of Christian music, but I could not deny the spiritual change. That would become the first step in my spiritual journey that has led to this book. God bless you, Sylvia.

Over the next few months, God began to wean me off today's music. For me, that was not an easy task, but for the Almighty, it was simple. He continued to bring Christian musicians into my life and they would share different Christian artists' music with me. I eventually "chose" Christian music instead of the garbage the world was doling out.

I later went on to Bible college and began to preach. At that time, I just spoke of my life and the effects that music had on it. Little did I know the impact my message would have. The first time I shared my testimony of how God had changed my life was at a Messenger College chapel service. God used that event to achieve dramatic results. When I finished preaching, an altar call was given, and up came the students. One of them even ran across the street to the dorms, and grabbed her music collection first. She then proceeded to smash every CD. Another student followed, then another, and another, until the equivalent of three egg boxes were filled with broken CDs, tapes, posters, pictures and other things pertaining to modern music. My ministry had begun.

Popular music has power, extreme power. It affected me in many ways, most notably through the "eyes." I guarantee popular music has also influenced you and your family to some extent. Whether in the past or present, mildly or extensively, you owe it to yourself, and more importantly, to God, to read and ask yourself the question, "Has it affected me?"

Satan has assumed a purpose on earth. Look at how the Bible describes him. He is called:

> "accuser of our brothers" (Rv 12:10)
> "that ancient serpent" (Rv 12:9)
> "your enemy" (1 Pt 5:8)
> "the evil one" (Mt 13:19)
> "the father of lies" (Jn 8:44)
> "the god of this age" (2 Cor 4:4)
> "the great dragon" (Rv 12:9)
> "a murderer" (Jn 8:44)
> "the one who leads the whole world astray"
>   (Rv 12:9)
> "prince of this world" (Jn 12:31)
> "the spirit at work in those who are disobedient"
>   (Eph 2:2)
> "the tempter" (Mt 4:3) [1]

This portrays a grim picture of satan's character and activities.

If we go back to Genesis, chapter 3, to that familiar scene in the garden, we will find in verse 1 that the serpent was more subtle then any beast the Lord God had made. After conducting a study on the word *subtle* in this particular text, I found that it means crafty in a negative sense. The devil was slick with Eve, and is still slick in his attempts to lead man astray.

In verse 5, the serpent says, "For God knows that in the day you eat of it that your eyes will be opened, and you will be like God, knowing good and evil." What the serpent was saying to her was this: You can do your own thing! You can follow your own will! You do not have to listen to anyone! Do what you want!! Do what brings you pleasure, or money, or fame. He was saying "Do what thou wilt."

The serpent, or satan, is portrayed as the one who shapes the world's system of thought. He induces mankind to follow their fleshly lusts, causing them to believe lies, and in turn blinding them to the power of the Gospel. He also stimulates opposition to God's work by directly attacking Christians and inspiring others to do so. Alongside of satan are his demons, who were booted out of heaven with him.

If we take a look at the book of Ezekiel, it can be noted that in 28:1-10 Ezekiel describes the pride of Ithobal II, who was ruler of Tyre at that time. But Ezekiel now moves beyond the earthly scene and describes for us the creation and then fall of a non-human, angelic creature. He is talking about satan himself, the real force behind the wickedness of Tyre. This is not the only time God speaks to satan through indirect source.

For example:
   1. He spoke to satan via the serpent (Gn 3:14,15)
   — "So the Lord God said the serpent . . . "
   2. God spoke to the devil through Peter (Mt 16:23)
   — "But He turned and said to Peter, Get behind Me, satan!" [2]

Now in describing the characteristics of this force, Ezekiel says in verse 12: "You were the seal of perfection, Full of wisdom and perfect in beauty." No man is ever described in these terms, but rather the opposite! (See Rom 3:23, which reads, "for all have sinned and fall short of the glory of God.") The writer goes on in Ezekiel 28:13: "You were in Eden, the garden of God; Every precious stone was your covering, . . ." Some have speculated that the author was speaking of Adam here, but the Bible nowhere speaks of Adam's being dressed in jewels or perfect in any way. [3]

Ezekiel continues, "the workmanship of thy tabrets and of thy pipes was prepared in thee in the day that thou was created." (Verse 13, as translated by the King James Version.)

Dr. J. Dwight Pentecost writes the following in reference to that passage: "Musical instruments were originally designed to be means of praising and worshiping God. It was not necessary for Lucifer to learn to play a musical instrument to praise God. If you please, he had a built-in pipe organ, or, he was an organ . . . Lucifer didn't have to look for someone to play the organ so that he could sing the doxology — he was a doxology." [4]

Let me repeat: Verse 13 reads that the musical instruments were "in thee." Not around thee, or near thee, or for thee, but IN THEE. Lucifer was a living, moving organ. When he waved his arms or walked or jumped, he would literally breathe out praises to God.

Ezekiel 28:14 continues, "Thou art the anointed cherub that covereth . . ." Theologically, the anointing of God is creative in nature. Remember that Jesus is the Messiah. The word Messiah is the Old Testament equivalent for Christ. Both Messiah and Christ mean "Anointed One." Jesus is also the Creator. Remember, John 1:3 tells us, "All things were made by Him; and without Him was not anything made that was made." So Jesus, the Christ (Anointed One), is the Creator. Jesus was also the most creative person to ever walk the earth. So the anointing has a creative element to it. Ezekiel explains that Lucifer was "the" anointed cherub. No other angel had that distinction. Lucifer had a creative anointing to emanate beautiful music.

What I propose to you is the following: The devil uses several vices today to lure man away from God. To name a few of the bigger ones, he uses alcohol, drugs, and sexual intercourse outside the bonds of a God-ordained marriage. In the realm of alcohol, the devil has the government fighting him with laws stating minors cannot have it, and that adults may only consume a certain amount before driving. There are also groups like Alcoholics Anonymous, Mothers Against Drunk Driving, and various others waging war on the enemy's use of alcohol.

As far as the war on drugs, the government arrests people for its use and distribution, and there are awareness groups fighting the devil's influence. Many are also stepping up to challenge the problem of promiscuity and premarital sex. Teaching abstinence is gaining ground in our local schools. Churches realize the destructive nature of lust and fornication, and congregations across this nation are praying against these evil vices.

Then there is today's popular music. As a general rule, it promotes a life of hedonism. Most modern music advocates rebellion, drinking, drugs, premarital sex, crime, selfishness, and a general do-what-you-want attitude. At least one biblical scholar (so far) agrees with me that satan is using popular music in today's world for his most subtle attack. The sad truth is, it is working. The reason is that there is virtually no opposition whatsoever to fight the music industry. Satan is running rampant and roaring like a lion. He is stealing the lives of American youth and pulling the hearts of our adults away from God. Before you read the last page of this book, it is my sincere hope and prayer that you also will join in this fight.

Lucifer is no stranger to the power music has over generations of people. He is the creative and powerful force behind popular music and I will demonstrate how he has strategically used it as a means to draw man away from God. I want to present you with the facts, and I want you to play the part of the jury. I will show you compelling evidence that will link our suspect, satan, to the "crime" I am accusing him of. I pray that your eyes will be opened to the truth, and as we sort through the facts, and the fingerprints become clearer, I believe you will arrive at the appropriate verdict — guilty.

1. Lawrence O. Richards, Ph.D., *The Revell Bible Dictionary* (Grand Rapids, Michigan: Fleming H. Revell, a division of Baker Book House, 1990), 896.
2. Dr. H. L. Willmington, *Willmington's Guide to the Bible* (Wheaton, Illinois: Tyndale House Publishers, Inc., 1984) 216.
3. Ibid.
4. Ibid.

Chapter 4

ALEISTER CROWLEY

Edward Alexander (Aleister) Crowley was born in England on October 12, 1875. His parents were members of a strict fundamentalist Christian sect called the Plymouth Brethren. Crowley grew up with a strong Bible background that eventually grew into a disdain for Christianity. He attended Trinity College at Cambridge University, dropping out just before he received his degree. A short time later, he was introduced to the Hermetic Order of the Golden Dawn. It was an occult society, led by S.L. MacGregor Mathers, that taught "magick, qabalah, alchemy, tarot, astrology, and other hermetic subjects." [1]

In 1898, Crowley was initiated into the Golden Dawn. In 1900, the group broke up. Crowley then began to travel extensively in the East, and there he learned the practice and mysticism of yoga. He incorporated western style magic with the oriental mysticism. [2] Through old friends and new acquaintances, Crowley joined a group called the Ordo Templi Orientis (O.T.O.). This group of high-ranking Freemasons claimed to have "discovered the supreme secret of practical magick." Crowley eventually took over, and began to organize it around the "Law of Thelema." His group became independent from the Freemasons (although based on the same patterns) and membership was opened to both sexes and those who were not Freemasons. [3]

Thelema is a Greek word that means "will" or "intention." It also is the name for a spiritual philosophy that is being established throughout the world. It came to fruition in the early part of the 20th century when it was developed by Aleister Crowley. Crowley declared that the world had entered a new age that will bring about change in the consciousness of humanity. [4]

Crowley married Rose Kelly in 1903. The couple went to Egypt for their honeymoon. In early 1904, Rose (who until this point showed no interest or desire for the occult) "began entering trance states and insisting to her husband that the 'god' Horus was trying to contact him."

The skeptical Crowley took Rose to the Boulak Museum to see if she could identify Horus for him.

She pointed to *The Stele of Revealing*, an Egyptian painted wooden tablet from the 26th dynasty depicting Horus receiving a sacrifice from the deceased . . ." Crowley was thoroughly impressed that the museum had labeled the piece with the number 666. He had identified with the number since childhood. In fact, he preferred to be called the Great Beast 666. [5]

Soon after discovering *The Stele of Revealing*, Crowley began to have contact with a "shadowy presence." On three successive days in April 1904, Crowley entered a room at noon and wrote down what the "shadowy presence" said as it stood beside him. The result was what he calls *Liber Al vel Legis* or *The Book of the Law*. This book "heralded the dawning of the new aeon of Horus, which was to be governed by the "Law of Thelema." [6]

Crowley's *The Book of the Law* has three chapters and 220 verses. Verses from the book include: "The word of the law is Thelema"; "I am the snake that giveth knowledge to worship me"; "Take whine (sic) and strange drugs whereof I will tell my prophet"; and the most famous verse, "Do what thou wilt shall be the whole of the law." Crowley dedicated his life to the advancement of Thelema, which includes several works and writings on magic, mysticism, yoga, Qabalah, and other occult subjects. Thelema says that "everyone has their own destiny, and that each is responsible for finding and fleshing out that destiny." It also says, "The only sin is restriction." [7]

Aleister Crowley is referred to as "the founding father of modern satanism." "He was known to practice ritual child sacrifice regularly" in support of his role as the devil's high priest or "magus." Crowley met death in 1947, finally succumbing to his huge heroine addiction. Before his death, Crowley started satanic covens in several U.S. cities, including Hollywood. Below are a few of his quotes. [8]

> I do not wish to argue that the doctrines of Jesus, they and they alone, have degraded the world to

its present condition. I take it that Christianity is not only the cause but the symptom of slavery. [9]

> That religion they call Christianity; the devil they honor they call God. I accept these definitions, as a poet must do, if he is to be at all intelligible to his age, and it is their God and their religion that I HATE and will Destroy. [10]

To close this section on Aleister Crowley, let us look at a few descriptions of some of Crowley's pagan services.

> Then came the slow, monotonous chant of the high priest. There is no good, evil is good. All hail, Prince of the world, to whom even God himself has given dominion . . . Men and women danced about leaping and swaying to the whining of infernal and discordant music. They sang obscene words . . . Women tore their bodices; some partially disrobed. One fair worshiper, seizing up the high priest's dagger, wounded herself in the breasts. At this all seemed to go madder then ever. [11]

In 1916, Crowley introduced a ritual to banish the "dying God" of Christianity, and he became one of the first to coin the term "new aeon" or "new age." Central to it was a frog that was baptized, worshiped, and then crucified, with the words "Lo, Jesus of Nazareth, how thou art taken in my snare. All my life thou hast plagued and affronted me . . . I blot thee out from the earth . . . thine aeon is passed; the Age of Horus is arisen by the Magick of the master, the great Beast that is Man, and his number is six, six, six." After mocking the Crucifixion, Crowley's law read, "Do what thou wilt shall be the whole of the law." [12] The frog was then killed with ". . . the dagger of art" while saying the words, "Into my hands I receive thy spirit." [13]

One of the arenas where Crowley has had his greatest impact is in the world of rock 'n' roll. Several bands, including the Black Crowes, Marilyn Manson, Mudvayne and David Bowie have connections to

Crowley. The bass player from the band 311 has Crowley's tree of life design tattooed on his back. Artists Darryl Hall, Sting and Jimmy Page studied Crowley and embraced aspects of his magical system. Page bought an occult bookstore and named it after a Crowley periodical — *The Equinox*. [14]

Page even has his own link to a Web site dedicated to Aleister Crowley. And he bought Crowley's house on the infamous Loch Ness and inscribed "Do what thou wilt" on the run off vinyl (the space on a vinyl record where the grooves end and the needle "runs off" toward the middle) for the first pressing of the album Led Zeppelin III. Page has been quoted as saying, "I've employed his (Crowley's) system in my own day to day life." [15]

1. http://www.crystalinks.com/crowley.html, 1-2.
2. http://www.crystalinks.com/crowley.html, 2.
3. http://www.mt.net/~watcher/crowleyalienlam.html,
4. http://www.crystalinks.com/crowley.html, 2-3.
5. http://www.crystalinks.com/crowley.html, 3.
6. http://www.crystalinks.com/crowley.html, 2.
7. http://www.crystalinks.com/crowley.html, 3-5.
8. Donald Phau, "The Satanic Roots of Rock," http://www.av1611.org/othpubls/roots.html, 4.
9. "Aleister Crowley, The World's Tragedy," XXXIX, quoted in Donald Phau, "The Satanic Roots of Rock," Dial-the-Truth Ministries Addendum, http://www.av1611.org/othpubls/roots.html, 6.
10. "Aleister Crowley, The World's Tragedy," XXXI, quoted in Donald Phau, "The Satanic Roots of Rock," Dial-the-Truth Ministries Addendum, http://www.av1611.org/othpubls/roots.html, 6
11. John Symonds, *The Great Beast: The Autobiography of Aleister Crowley*, (New York, New York:Roy Publisher, 1952) 124, 125.
12. John Symonds, *The Great Beast*, 132-134.
13. Ibid.
14. Eric Holmberg, *Hell's Bells 2: The Dangers of Rock 'n' Roll* (Brentwood, TN: Reel 2 Real Ministries, 2001), video.
15. Paul Kendall and Dave Lewis, *Led Zeppelin: In Their Own Words* (Omnibus Press, 1981) 103, quoted in *Hell's Bells 2: The Dangers of Rock 'n' Roll* (Brentwood, TN: Reel 2 Real Ministries, 2001).

Chapter 5

HOOKED

> "Head bangers in leather
> Sparks fly in the dead of the night . . .
> The beast is ready to devour
> All the metal they can hold . . .
> We've got up front fanatics
> Tearing down the barricade
> To reach the stage
> Can you feel the rage
> It's your one way ticket to midnight
> Call it Heavy Metal."
>
> "Heavy Metal" by Sammy Hagar
> (www.lyricsdownload.com)

As a junior high student, you have goals. You want to score touchdowns during noon hour recess. You want to have a girlfriend so you can ignore her. You want to make it to class just seconds before the bell rings (or in my case, a few seconds after). But most importantly, you want to sneak into the senior high school and try to mix in with your role models.

I had been to numerous high school sporting events and watched my heroes. I had been attending senior high dances since sixth grade (my parents were chaperones). I had snuck down to the senior high candy counter and bought candy with my dad. I had even practiced with the varsity basketball team. But nothing would compare to this day.

The junior high was going to the Senior Variety Show at the high school. We were going to get to rub elbows with the stars. For us, this might as well have been Hollywood. We were going to see the people that we looked up to (and those we were afraid of) perform on stage.

I can remember only a three-and-a-half minute span of the entire show. It was the first act, and most definitely the first hook that satan set in my little rock 'n' roll heart. The large curtain parted. The light show began, shooting all imaginable colors throughout the auditorium. Then we heard it — Sammy Hagar's screeching guitar. Pandemonium was about to begin.

Every hair on my body stood up as they played the song "Heavy Metal" loud enough to shake the room. I was standing in amazement. Then my hands went up, my feet began to move, and I began to scream. For those three-and-a-half minutes, I forgot my name, my cares, and my inhibitions. I was riding in a state of euphoria. It is hard to explain, but I literally felt like my head was going to explode.

I had experienced the joy of watching my favorite team win. I had felt the joy of receiving back my note with the word "yes" circled, accompanied by a line of "Xs and Os." I had even felt the joy of being loved unconditionally by my family. But I had never felt this. The music took me away. It transported me to a place that was unattainable by any other means. To put it simply, I was "high" and I needed to feel it again.

The seniors were only doing "mock rock" that day. I don't know if any one of them even knew how to play an instrument, but it did not matter to me. I wanted it. I wanted that euphoric feeling back. I wanted that rush. Mine was not the only heart stirred. In fact, five of us could not wait until our own Senior Variety Show to repeat the event ourselves. That day came, but that's another chapter.

My life had changed. That was the day I put aside my baseball glove. That was the day I let go of my moral standards. That was the day I set myself on a course to destruction. I wanted to sing. I wanted to "bang my head." I wanted to be a rock star. I wanted "heavy metal."

"You shall have no other gods before Me."
Exodus 20:3

Chapter 6

KENNETH ANGER

The second subject I want to present into evidence is a follower of Aleister Crowley named Kenneth Anger. Like Aleister Crowley, Anger is a satanic priest or "Magus." Anger was only 17 when Crowley died in 1947, but he was already making films that "which even by today's standards, reek of pure evil." [1]

Maury Terry, an investigator, wrote a book called *Ultimate Evil: An Investigation into a Dangerous Satanic Cult*. In his book, Terry states that Anger is a key link between the Process Church, which is a satanic cult, and the rock and roll group the Rolling Stones. He reports that in 1966-67, the Process Church was recruiting in London, and that Anger was also present. [2] One author states that Rolling Stones' singer Mick Jagger and guitarist Keith Richards, and their girlfriends Marianne Faithfull and Anita Pallenburg "listened spellbound as Anger turned them on to Crowley's powers and ideas." [3]

Anger was in London working on a film called *Lucifer Rising*. It was dedicated to Aleister Crowley. The film fielded a team of very key people. It included players from the Process Church, the Rolling Stones and the Charles Manson family cult. Any guesses as to who composed the music for the film? It was Mick Jagger. Oh, the cast gets better. The part of Lucifer was played by Bobby Beausoleil. Beausoleil was a member of Charles Manson's gang and reportedly Anger's homosexual lover. [4]

A few months into the film, Beausoleil returned to California to carry out the first of the Manson family murders. He was later arrested, and is now serving time with his leader, Charles Manson. With his lover gone, Anger chose Anton LaVey, the author of *The Satanic Bible* and the head of the First Church of Satan, to play Lucifer. The filmed was released in 1969 with a different title. It was called *Invocation to My Demon Brother*. [5]

Anger, while in London, was also successful in recruiting Anita Pallenburg to the Process Church. One of the Rolling Stones' friends, Tony Sanchez, writes of

Pallenburg in his book *Up and Down with the Rolling Stones*:

> She was obsessed with black magic and began to carry a string of garlic with her everywhere — even to bed — to ward off vampires. She also had a strange mysterious old shaker for holy water, which she used for some of her rituals. Her ceremonies became increasingly secret, and she warned me never to interrupt her when she was working on a spell. [6]

Sanchez continues:

> In her bedroom she kept a huge, ornate, carved chest, which she guarded so jealously that I assumed it was her drug stash. The house was empty one day, and I decided to take a peep inside. The drawers were filled with scraps of bone, wrinkled skin and fur from strange animals. [7]

In 1967, while under the influence of Anger and the Process Church, the Rolling Stones released their first album giving praise to their god, entitled *Their Satanic Majesties Request*. The album cover pictures a tarot card designed by Crowley. [8]

The Rolling Stones' rise to fame was closely related to the rock 'n' roll group called the Beatles. The intention was to portray the two bands as opposites. The Beatles were clean-cut, and the Stones, as they were called, were to be "dirty" and "rebellious." Author Donald Phau states that the Stones' first hit record was actually written by the Beatles, and that Beatle George Harrison "set up the arrangements for their first recording contract." [9]

Phau claims that the Stones followed the same path as the Beatles such as appearing on England's television show *Thank Your Lucky Stars* and America's *Ed Sullivan Show*. He claims that the Stones' appearance received a much different reaction. While the Beatles were loved, the Stones were abhorred. [10]

The gimmick had worked. The Rolling Stones' manager, Andrew Oldham, was elated at the response. He told the group, "We're going to make you exactly the opposite to those nice, clean, tidy Beatles. And the more the parents hate you, the more the kids will love you. Just wait and see." [11] The publicity was exactly what was wanted. Within a few months, the group's records were selling millions of copies.

Phau states:

> The "rock stars" are totally artificial media creations. Their public image, as well as their music, is fabricated from behind the scenes by controllers. For example, when the Beatles first arrived in the U.S. in 1964, they were mobbed at the airport by hundreds of screaming teenage girls. The national press immediately announced "Beatlemania" had besieged the U.S.A. But the girls had all been transported from a girls' school in the Bronx, and paid for their screaming performance by Beatle promoters. [12]

I agree with Phau that the music is fabricated by a controller and the bands are pathetic puppets. Their ultimate controller is satan. The Stones have been openly singing about the devil and displaying his fruits in their lifestyles for over 30 years. Yet today they are packing stadiums, writing new albums, and partying on. They are anointed by someone, and it is surely not the Savior of the world, Jesus Christ. How else could they still be attracting a cultlike following, while being worshiped as if they themselves were gods?

Anyone who knows anything about the Stones knows of their trademark lips with the tongue sticking out. Mick Jagger himself states that he based that logo on the "fake" goddess "Kali," who is known to stick out her tongue. [13]

Isaiah 57:3-4 reminds us:

"But come here,
You sons of the sorceress,
You offspring of the adulterer and the harlot!
Whom do you ridicule?
Against who do you make a wide mouth
And stick out the tongue? . . . "

Connected or not? Coincidence or not, you must admit it is profoundly strange. Between 1963 and 1964, the Beatles and the Rolling Stones attacked Western Europe and American culture. The arrival of these two English groups in the U.S. was well-planned and well-timed. America was in an uproar over the assassination of President John F. Kennedy, not to mention the mass civil rights movement being led by Martin Luther King, Jr. [14]

In 1968 and 1969, the U.S. and Europe witnessed mass strikes of students and workers. Huge outdoor music concerts were used to put a spin on the growing discontent of the population. These concerts were also used as vehicles for a major promotion of the drug-saturated, free sex way of life. For millions of concert-goers, thousands of tablets of the hallucinogenic drug LSD were made freely accessible. For the past 40 years "Western society has been under the gun of a deliberate plan of cultural warfare, with the purpose of eliminating Judeo-Christian civilization." [15] One writer stated: "The plan was now to use both the Beatles and the Rolling Stones as the means to transform an entire generation into heathen followers of the New Age, followers which could be molded into the future cadre of a satanic movement and then deployed into our schools, law enforcement agencies and political leadership." [16]

---

1. Donald Phau, "The Satanic Roots of Rock," http://www.av1611.org/othpubls/roots.html, 4.
2. Ibid.
3. Tony Sanchez, *Up and Down with the Rolling Stones*, 155, quoted in Donald Phau, "The Satanic Roots of Rock," http://www.av1611.org/othpubls/roots.html, 4.
4. Phau, "The Satanic Roots of Rock," 5.
5. Ibid.

6. Sanchez, *Up and Down with the Rolling Stones*, 159 quoted in Donald Phau, "The Satanic Roots of Rock," http://www.av1611.org/othpubls/roots.html, 4., .
7. Ibid.
8. Phau, "The Satanic Roots of Rock," 5.
9. Phau, "The Satanic Roots of Rock," 3.
10. Phau, "The Satanic Roots of Rock," 4.
11. Sanchez, *Up and Down with the Rolling Stones*, 17, quoted in Donald Phau, "The Satanic Roots of Rock," http://www.av1611.org/othpubls/roots.html, 4.
12. Phau, "The Satanic Roots of Rock," 1.
13. Eric Holmberg, *Hell's Bells 2: The Dangers of Rock 'n' Roll* (Brentwood, TN: Reel 2 Real Ministries, 2001), video.
14. Phau, "The Satanic Roots of Rock," 2.
15. Ibid.
16. Donald Phau, "The Satanic Roots of Rock," Dial-the-Truth Ministries Addendum, http://www.av1611.org/othpubls/roots.html, 4.

Chapter 7

DOMINOES

"There's a picture in the gallery of a
Fallen angel looked a lot like you
We forget where we come from sometimes . . .
You don't have to die to go to heaven
Or hang around to be born again
Just tune into what this place has got to offer
Cause we may never be here again . . .
We can have the best of both worlds a little
Heaven right here on earth ."

"Best of Both Worlds" by Van Halen
(http://www.yimpan.com/Songsite/Lyric/index.asp?sid=841)

    Click, click, click. One falls into another, and then faster and faster they fall down. Once you set up one in front of another, all it takes is a little push. Countless times I had set up those dominoes as a child just to watch them fall, and I found myself laughing through every minute of it.
    At the age of 15, I was like most other curious adolescents. I wanted to belong and be accepted by my peers. So I often went along with the group and did things just to fit in, even though I knew better. I vividly remember one winter night during my freshman year. Jimmy, Shane, Billy Doby and I were headed to Shane's house for the night. We had found a "buyer" and it was time to party. Yukon Jack would be attending the show and providing the euphoric sense of freedom. Yukon and 7-Up. It would be my first and last encounter.
    As we jammed to the songs "Panama" and "Jump," Shane, Jimmy and Billy were outside in the Michigan winter, in their underwear, sliding down snowbanks. I was guarding the booze. I hung on with a death grip that would last for the next 15 years. Well, why not? Especially when you are listening to AC/DC's "Have a Drink on Me," and Ozzy Osbourne's "Suicide Solution" that contains the words, "Take a bottle and drown your sorrows." It was a quick answer to a long-standing problem.

A lot of firsts took place that night — my first drink, my first drunk, my first binge and my first drunken vomit. Later, it became my first hangover. In my eyes, I had become a man.

Then came my sophomore year, which brought greater depths of sin with it. I played football that year, and although that was not a sin, with my bony frame it should have been. When you are 6 feet 2 inches tall, and weigh 167 pounds, you are not made to play football. I played to be accepted, and hated every minute of it. I was more concerned with the dances that followed the games and arranging the alcohol deliveries.

Getting alcohol was never, ever a problem. There was usually a "buyer," and when there wasn't, we stole it. We went to great lengths to set up our thefts, and were very successful. We would literally map out the routes of beer trucks, wait until the driver went inside, and then unload his truck into ours. When that became too risky, we started stealing directly from stores. Nothing was going to stop us from drinking.

Each game would be a quick loss, a quick shower (if needed), and a quick trip to the parking lot. There we would slam booze as fast as possible, and then chew an entire pack of Hubba-Bubba bubblegum. We would pay and enter the dance, passing by the principal, vice-principal and a host of teachers. They knew. They had to. We reeked of booze and acted like idiots. The plain and simple fact was that they did not care.

Between the ages of 14 and 18 you want to be inspired. I call them the "growth" years (see more in chapter 17, entitled "Stunted Growth"). The choices made at this stage will impact the rest of your life. At 14, I was most interested in the Detroit Tigers' score, what my Dad was doing, and getting someone to play catch. At 17, after four years of influence by music that pushed drinking and carousing, my concerns became Ozzy's new album, having beer money, and finding an available girl to fulfill my needs.

Things got worse. In my desperate need for attention and acceptance, I found it by being a little "on the edge." I found satisfaction in watching pornography, reading

The Satanic Bible, telling others about Lucifer (satan), and scheming on how to date the next pretty face.

I thought rock and roll, I talked rock and roll, and I lived rock and roll. I loved the fact that the popular bands sang about alcohol and the satisfaction you could obtain from a woman. Songs about perverse sex acts were increasing, unannounced to parents, as they were usually written in adolescent code words. Although many music genres now simply sing their obscene thoughts, the "pop" music culture is still using these "codes" today (ie. "pop," "rockin'," "shoot," "swinging," and "score," are used to symbolize sex).

Our school was infiltrated with rock and roll. We played it at lunch, in gym class, and even in some classrooms. Girls and guys alike banged their heads, and thrust their hips in and out. You might or might not find it surprising, but the young girls were as obsessed with drinking, sex, and sharing conquests as if they were men at a seedy bar. The days of the "shy, innocent girl" were becoming the days of the "hoochie mama," and for the most part, the boys were loving it.

Why were we changing? The music. I will address this in greater lengths in other chapters, but we were being bombarded with ideas about promiscuity. A few examples would include Samantha Fox's *song* "I Wanna Have Some Fun" ("and work my body all night long"). Another song would be one by the band Divinyls called "I Touch Myself." The female lead of the trashy ensemble sings in her heavy-breathed voice the words, "I don't want anybody else, and when I think about you, I touch myself . . . I honestly do, I touch myself."

Popular music was a light in the darkness to me. When I was out desperately searching for something to believe in, something to trust in, and something to stimulate me, I found music. Whether I was drinking to AC/DC, smoking pot to Ozzy Osbourne, having sex to Prince, or banging my head to Metallica, I had something to believe in. The music tumbled into alcohol, alcohol tumbled into pornography, pornography tumbled into *The Satanic Bible,* which tumbled into demonic powers, which tumbled into sex, which tumbled into drugs, and the devil was laughing all the way.

"But each one is tempted when he is drawn away by his own desires and enticed. Then, when desire has conceived, it gives birth to sin; and sin, when it is full grown, brings forth death."

James 1:14-15

Chapter 8

ALDOUS HUXLEY

Yes, another band, and another link to the devil. I now wish to present you with the third subject, and describe the impact he had on the group the Doors. His name is Aldous Huxley.

Aldous Huxley (1894-1963) was a well-known British writer. His books are currently used in the California public school system. What Huxley might not be as well-known for is his experimentation with psychotropic drugs. He supported their use as a "tool of enlightenment."

One of Huxley's writings is called *The Doors of Perception and Heaven and Hell*. It is considered by some to be a classic of psychedelic literature. Approximately 10 years after its release, "the Doors" became the name of a band.

The Doors' keyboardist, Ray Manzarek, had the following quote about his band:

> At the time, we had been ingesting a lot of psychedelic chemicals, so the doors of perception were cleansed in our minds, and we saw the music as a vehicle to, in a sense, become proselytizers of a new religion, a religion of self, of each man as God. That was the original idea behind the Doors . . . [1]

Jim Morrison, former lead singer for the rock group the Doors, died mysteriously on July 3, 1971. Morrison was involved in the occult. He and his wife were married at a Wicca ceremony. During the ceremony, the two stood in a pentagram and drank each other's blood. [2] Morrison once gave reference to the fact that satan was responsible for his thoughts and possibly his music. He stated, "I met the Spirit of Music . . . An appearance of the devil in a Venice canal. Running, I saw a satan, or Satyr, moving beside me, a fleshy shadow of my secret mind . . . " [3]

Manzarek had this to say about Morrison: "He was not a performer. He was not an entertainer. He was a shaman. He was possessed." [4] Band member Robbie Krieger stated, "We were revivalists as well as musicians and wanted our audience to undergo a religious experience." [5] Was their religious experience in the name of Jesus? Here are some clues.

On the back cover of the Doors' album, entitled *13*, is a picture of the group gathered around a bust of one Aleister Crowley. What did Huxley, the man who inspired the Doors, think about being moral and following Jesus? Well let's look at his own words:

> For myself, as no doubt for most of my contemporaries, the philosophy of meaninglessness was essentially an instrument of liberation. The liberation we desired was from a certain system of morality. We objected to the morality because it interfered with our sexual freedom. [6]

Huxley ingested psilocybin mushrooms with a man named Timothy Leary. Leary recalls one of the times in the following statement: "Huxley's eyes were closed. Suddenly he clapped his hands. 'Your role is quite simple. Become a cheerleader for evolution. That's what I did and my grandfather before me. These brain drugs will bring about vast changes in society. We (must) . . . spread the word. The obstacle to this evolution, Timothy, is the Bible.' " [7]

I have no further questions for Huxley.

---

1. Andrew Doe and John Tobler, *The Doors in Their Own Words* (London: Omnibus Press, 1988), 13, quoted in Eric Holmberg, *Hell's Bells 2: The Dangers of Rock 'n' Roll*, 2001, Reel 2 Real Ministries, video.
2. Donald Phau, "The Satanic Roots of Rock," Dial-the-Truth Ministries Addendum, http://www.av1611.org/othpubls/roots.html, 8.
3. Frank Lisciandro, *Wilderness: The Lost Writings of Jim Morrison, Volume 1* (New York: Random House and Vintage Books, 1988), 36-38, quoted in Donald Phau, "The Satanic Roots of Rock, "Dial-

the-Truth Ministries Addendum, http://www.av1611.org/othpubls/roots.html.
4. Pamela Des Barres, *Rock Bottom* (UK: Time Warner Books, 208, quoted in Holmberg, Hell's Bells 2, video.
5. Eric Holmberg, *Hell's Bells 2: The Dangers of Rock 'n' Roll*, (Brentwood, Tn., Reel 2 Real Ministries, 2001) video..
6. Aldous Huxley, *Ends and Means* (London: Chatto & Windus, 1946), 273, quoted in Holmberg, Hell's Bells 2, video.
7. Timothy Leary, *Flashbacks* (Jeremy Tarcher, Inc., 1983) 44, quoted in Holmberg, *Hell's Bells 2*, video.

Chapter 9

INNOCULATED

> "Run for the hills
> We're both sinners and saints
> Not a woman, but a whore
> I can just taste the hate".
>
> "Too Young To Fall In Love" by Motley Crue
> (www.lyricsdepot.com)

The year was *1984* and so was the album. Van Halen was the "bomb" and they enjoyed dehumanizing women in their lyrics. They told women to give them a try in their song "Jump"; they had their date "reach down, between my legs, ease the seat back" in the song "Panama"; and they said to their object of affection that her "giant butt makes me scream" in the song "Drop Dead Legs". It did not stop there.

Van Halen also sang the self-explanatory song "Hot for Teacher" and "House of Pain." The latter contained the lyrics, "Say you're gonna leave me 'cause I only tie you up. Always love you tender but you only like it rough." Other popular songs at the time included "Legs" by the band ZZ Top, which contained the lyrics ". . . and she knows how to use them." I was afraid to date a woman, but I certainly was forming an opinion of what she was going to be like and what she was going to do.

Motley Crue had written a song that became my favorite. It was called "Too Young To Fall In Love." This song would stick with me for years. There came a point where I no longer wanted a woman, I simply wanted the whore. That is what the song proclaimed, and it was what I longed for. I had listened to so much mind-conditioning lyrics, watched so many seductive MTV videos, and read so many eye-opening rock band interviews, that at the age of 14, I was hooked. I wanted to have sex, and when I had it, it was going to be all about me.

The music had me believing "she" would be very attractive, wear skimpy clothes and heavy make-up, and would obey my every command. I set out looking for her.

She was not hard to find. The girls were watching the same videos and listening to the same lyrics. They were being pushed to wear skimpy fashions, act dumb, drink to lose their inhibitions, and believe that they would have to provide sex to keep their man.

I grew up in the smallest county in the state of Michigan. It is full of farms and very small towns. The only forms of entertainment at our age was to go to the movies, get drunk, and have sex. I would say roughly 75 percent of the kids participated in all of the above. It was not confined to the big cities; it was a nationwide epidemic.

The epidemic began before we were even born. It was tearing down the morals of our nation. The evilest of men know that if you want to change the values of a nation, you start with the minds of the youth. Popular music had invaded America in the mid-sixties and had been providing a healthy dose of immoral brainwashing. A generation of young people would progress from thinking immorally to becoming amoral. The concept of absolute truth was eroding in the world, and it is on its deathbed today. "Do what thou wilt" was beginning to establish a foothold in our young lives. We were being reared as children of the devil, and we didn't even know it.

> **"When you were slaves of sin, you didn't have to please God. But what good did you receive from the things you did? All you have to show for them is your shame, and they lead to death. Now you have been set free from sin, and you are God's slaves. This will make you holy and will lead you to eternal life . . . "**
> **Romans 6:20-22**
> **(Contemporary English Version)**

Chapter 10

TIMOTHY LEARY

Enter subject number four. As some of you might have guessed, his name is Timothy Leary. Timothy Leary was a Harvard psychologist and professor. He preached that spiritual "enlightenment" could be obtained by using the drug LSD. (1)

In 1960, Leary went to Mexico and began to experiment with psilocybin mushrooms, "a substance that Aztec priests ingested to experience hallucinations." He reportedly received "a Niagara of sensory input" from the mushrooms and began to use them in his psychological research at Harvard. In 1962, Leary began to experiment with LSD. He became convinced that these drugs were the successful means of therapy for humans. (2)

Leary had a powerful effect on people of his generation. He stated himself, "My crime is the ancient and familiar one of corrupting the minds of youth. This charge is a valid one." (3) A charismatic and gifted speaker, Leary used these talents to attract many followers. He even described himself as a "40-year-old, smart-aleck, atheist Harvard professor." Eventually, his outlandish behavior caught up with him and Leary was fired by Harvard. Before this time, he had been handing out LSD to his Harvard student volunteers. (4)

Author Patrick Swift calls Leary the counterculture "poster boy" of the era. His famous quote was "turn on, tune in, and drop out." (5) I now want to share what that means, in Leary's words: "What I am saying happens to be the oldest method of humans wisdom — look within, find your own divinity, detach yourself from social and material struggle, turn on, tune in, and drop out . . . " (6) The message was about hedonism and rebellion. Swift says, "To tens of thousands of young people, he offered hope that the difficult personal and social issues of life could be changed via a chemically-created utopia." (7)

Any guesses of whom Leary was a very serious follower? Aleister Crowley. On PBS's *Late Night America*, Leary admitted to being an "admirer" of Crowley, and believed he was carrying on Crowley's work. He said, "Well I've been an admirer of Aleister Crowley. I think that I'm carrying on much of the work that he started over a hundred years ago . . . He was in favor of finding yourself, and 'do what thou wilt shall be the whole of the law' under love. It was a very powerful statement. I'm sorry he isn't around now to appreciate the glories he started." [8]

Leary then went one step further — he had an epiphany. In 1971, during a tarot card reading (using cards that Aleister Crowley had designed), he supposedly became "Crowley reborn, and (was) to complete the work Crowley began, preparing humanity for cosmic consciousness." [9] Leary even wrote to R.A. Wilson saying, " . . . the coincidences-synchronicities between my life and His (capital "H" is Leary's) are embarrassing." [10]

Leary expressed that "do whatever you want attitude." And he made plans to spread his "knowledge across the world." Leary set out to do this using the tool of rock and roll. He influenced John Lennon, Jefferson Airplane, the Grateful Dead and Jimi Hendrix, to name a few. He stated: " . . . I rejoice to see our culture being taken over by joyful young messiahs who dispel our fears and charm us back into the pagan dance of harmony." [11]

"Despite the many deaths and drug burnouts that ensued, Leary remained unrepentant and unremorseful to the end," writes Swift in his article. "Now, Timothy Leary is dead. *People* and *Rolling Stone* magazines heap glowing praise upon him." [12] Leary actually talked about God becoming incarnate in a particular band. He said, "He has come back as " . . . the four-sided mandala — the Beatles. The means by which to spread the new gospel — music. The sacrament — drugs." [13] Lennon used Leary's translation of *The Tibetan Book of the Dead* for the lyrics in the 1966 release "Tomorrow Never Knows."

One year later came the album *Sgt. Pepper's Lonely Hearts Club Band.* [14] *All Music Guide* claimed the Beatles' album *Sgt. Pepper* "will forever be known as the recording that changed rock and roll." *Time* magazine said *Sgt. Pepper* was "drenched in drugs." (15) The cover of The Beatle's *Sgt. Pepper* album shows the band with a backdrop of several people. Ringo Starr was quoted in *Hit Parader* magazine in October 1976 as saying they are people "we like and admire." Paul McCartney, also quoted in describing the cover, said, " . . . we were going to have photos on the wall of all our HEROS . . . " (16)

There are many infamous people in the picture on that album cover, including four Hindu priests and a man named Aldous Huxley. Second from the left, on the top row, is Alcister Crowley. Many people at that time did not even know who Aleister Crowley was, but the Beatles did. Chances are, you did not know who he was. He was a BABY MURDERER, and the Beatles considered him a hero. The Beatles were devout followers of Crowley. Beatle Lennon says in an interview, the "whole idea of the Beatles" was Crowley's infamous "do what thou wilt." "The whole Beatle idea was to do what you want, right? To take your own responsibility, do what you want and try not to harm other people, right? DO WHAT THOU WILT, as long as it doesn't hurt somebody . . . " (17)

> "They're COMPLETELY ANTI-CHRIST. I mean, I am anti-Christ as well, but they're so anti-Christ they shock me, which isn't an easy thing."
>
> — Derek Taylor, press officer for the Beatles (18)
>
> "Christianity will go, it will vanish and shrink. I needn't argue about that. I'm right and will be proved right . . . We're more popular than Jesus now." (19)

Author Donald Phau, in his article *The Satanic Roots of Rock*, said the Beatles were a group of four pathetic musicians who started their careers playing guitars for strippers in the slums of England and West Germany. He states that even in their first performances the Beatles were frequently high on a drug called Preludin. (20)

How had the Beatles gotten to this point? I'm glad you asked. Recording director George Martin molded them into what they became. He brought the Beatles in, had them scrubbed, washed, and their hair done into those memorable haircuts. Martin was a trained classical musician and a student of the London School of Music. At the time, the Fab Four could not play any instrument other then guitar. Furthermore, none of them could read music. [21] On their first hit record, "Love Me Do," a studio musician played drums in place of Ringo Starr. Martin stated Ringo "couldn't do a roll to save his life." Phau said that Martin would take what the Beatles gave him, and then turn it into the "hits" that are still played today. [22]

From the beginning, Beatlemania was a myth. In late 1963, while in London, the band made its first major television appearance. According to Phau, the next day's newspapers stated that fans, of up to 1,000 in number, were held back by police. Yet the pictures displayed in each newspaper was cropped so close that only three or four of the teens could be seen. A photographer who witnessed the event said, "There were no riots. I was there. We saw eight girls, even less then eight." [23] It was no more than a publicity stunt.

In February 1964, the myth of Beatlemania hit America with the previously mentioned airport setup. This landed the four a spot on the *Ed Sullivan Show* for an unprecedented two weeks in a row. There they shook their heads and bodies in a ritualistic way that would be copied by numerous rock groups. The strategy worked, the phenomenon of the Beatles was created. [24]

One month after the album's release, the Beatles shocked the world by announcing, publicly, that they were regularly taking LSD. Beatles' member Paul McCartney, in an interview with *Life* magazine said, "LSD opened my eyes. We only use one-tenth of our brain." They also publicly called for the legalization of marijuana. [25] The late Beatle George Harrison once said, "When I was younger, with the aftereffects of the LSD that opened something up inside of me in 1966, a flood of other thoughts came into my head which led me to the yogis." [26] Remember, one of the things Aleister Crowley taught was yoga.

Harrison embraced Krishna consciousness for "evangelic education" as Timothy Leary described it.

Krishna leader Muunda Goswami said to Harrison, "I don't think it is possible to calculate just how many people were turned on to Krishna consciousness by your song 'My Sweet Lord.'" [27] Harrison replied, "My idea in 'My Sweet Lord,' because it sounded like a pop song, was to sneak up on them (his audience) a bit. The point was to have the people not offended by 'hallelujah' and by the time it gets to 'Hare Krishna,' they're already hooked and their foot's tapping and they're already singing along . . . to lull them into a sense of false security." [28]

This subtle appeal that Harrison is talking about also works for influencing people to begin to accept perversity, the use of illicit drugs, promiscuity and the beliefs of Aleister Crowley.

In an interview with the homosexualist magazine *The Advocate*, pop singer Madonna acknowledged she is " . . . constantly trying to challenge the accepted ways of behaving sexually." [29] Responding to the blatant shows of homosexuality in her videos and concerts, and how it will affect the teenage youth, she says, "They digest it on a lot of different levels. Some people will see it and be disgusted by it, but maybe they'll be unconsciously aroused by it . . . If people keep seeing it and seeing it and seeing it, eventually it's not going to be such a strange thing." [30]

Remember, the devil is cunning. He slides in through the back door. He creeps into people's lives and then begins to erode morality, as in the examples above. We must be on constant guard against such attacks. If you doubt that such a scenario could be created by satan by using the satanic Church and other influences, you'll just have to keep on reading.

1. Donald Phau, "The Satanic Roots of Rock," Dial-the-Truth Ministries Addendum, http://www.av1611.org/othpubls/roots.html, 10.
2. Patrick Swift, "Timothy Leary's Dead," http://www.u-turn.net/4-3/leary.html, 1.
3. Ibid.
4. Swift, "Timothy Leary's Dead," 2.
5. Ibid.
6. Eric Holmberg, *Hell's Bells 2: The Dangers of Rock 'n' Roll*, 2001, Reel 2 Real Ministries, video.
7. Swift, "Timothy Leary's Dead," 2.

Rockin' Down

8. PBS' *Late Night America*, quoted in Holmberg, *Hells Bells 2*, video.
9. R.A. Wilson, *Cosmic Trigger* (New Falcon Publications, 1977) 116, quoted in Holmberg, *Hell's Bells 2*, video.
10. Holmberg, Hell's Bells 2: The Dangers of Rock 'n' Roll, 2001, Reel 2 Real Ministries, from R.A. Wilson "Cosmic Trigger" (New Falcon Publications, 1977) 103, video.
11. Holmberg, Hell's Bells 2: The Dangers of Rock 'n' Roll, 2001, Reel 2 Real Ministries
12. Swift, "Timothy Leary's Dead," 3.
13. Timothy Leary, "Thank God for the Beatles," quoted in Holmberg, Hell's Bells 2, video.
14. Holmberg, *Hell's Bells 2*, video.
15. Author unknown, "The All Music Guide", *Time*, Sept 26, 1967, 62, quoted in Phau, "The Satanic Roots Of Rock," Dial-the-Truth Ministries Addendum, http://www.av1611.org/othpubls/roots.html, 6.om.
16. Musician magazine, Special Collectors Edition, Beatles and Rolling Stones, 1988, 12, quoted in Phau, "The Satanic Roots Of Rock," Dial-the-Truth Ministries Addendum, http://www.av1611.org/othpubls/roots.html, 6.
17. David Sheff and G. Barry Golson, "The Playboy Interview with John Lennon & Yoko Ono," quoted in Phau, "The Satanic Roots Of Rock," Dial-the-Truth Ministries Addendum, http://www. av1611.org/othpubls/roots.html, 7.
18. *Saturday Evening Post*, Aug. 8, 1964, quoted in Phau, "The Satanic Roots Of Rock," Dial-the-Truth Ministries Addendum, http://www.av1611.org/othpubls/roots.html, pg. 7.
19. *San Francisco Chronicle*, April 13, 1966, 26, quoted in Phau, "The Satanic Roots Of Rock," Dial-the-Truth Ministries Addendum, http://www.av1611.org/othpubls/roots.html, pg. 7.
20. Phau, "The Satanic Roots Of Rock," http://www.av1611.org/othpubls/roots.html, 2.
21. Phau, "The Satanic Roots Of Rock," http://www.av1611.org/othpubls/roots.html, 3.
22. Ibid.
23. Ibid.
24. Ibid.
25. Phau, "The Satanic Roots Of Rock," http://www.av1611.org/othpubls/roots.html, 5.
26. Anthony Decurtis, *Rolling Stone*, 11/5/87, quoted in Holmberg, *Hell's Bells 2*, video.
27. A.C. Bhaktivedanta, *Chant and Be Happy: The Power of Mantra Meditation* (The Bhaktivedanta Book Trust, 1982), 32 , quoted in Holmberg, Hell's Bells 2, video.
28. A.C. Bhaktivedanta, *Chant and Be Happy: The Power of Mantra Meditation* (The Bhaktivedanta Book Trust, 1982), 32 , 34, quoted in Holmberg, Hell's Bells 2, video.
29. *The Advocate*, May 7, 1991.
30. Holmberg, *Hell's Bells 2*, video.

Chapter 11

TWISTED

"In the beginning
Good always overpowered the evils
Of all man's sins . . .
But in time
The nations grew weak
And our cities fell to slums
While evils stood strong
In the dusts of hell
Lurked the blackest of hates
For he whom they feared
Awaited them . . .
Now many, many lifetimes later
Lay destroyed, beaten, beaten down,
Only corpses of rebels
Ashes of dreams
And blood stained streets . . .
It has been written
(Those who have the youth
Have the future)
So come now children of the beast
Be strong
And Shout at the Devil."

"In the Beginning" by Motley Crue
(http://display.lyrics.astraweb.com) (sic)

"Shout, shout, shout, shout at the devil. Shout, shout, shout, shout at the devil." We must have listened to that tape 100 times over. Motley Crue was awesome, at least to a bunch of high schoolers. With make-up, long earrings, leather suits, and women everywhere, they were our heroes.

Satan would use this group to open a door into our hearts and also into our souls. This was Devil Class 101. This song was telling us that we were children of the beast, and satan was a "cool" thing. Forgive the slang, but "cool" was the word then and we wanted to be every part of it.

I appointed myself to research the Satanic Church and become the neighborhood authority on the subject. I went out and purchased *The Satanic Bible* (one-third of which is directly quoted from *The Equinox* written by

Aleister Crowley) and began to read. Of course the first chapter I turned to was the one about sex. This didn't intrigue me enough, so I began to skim the pages. I stopped at the part that described how to perform a ritual. I read about conducting a séance. It involved using a voluntary nude female and then performing a series of bizarre acts. I spread the word. People I knew actually wanted to participate, male and female alike. I remember becoming very enthralled with this book. I had bought it merely to create a reputation for myself, but now it was going deeper.

I wanted demonic power and I would meditate in hopes of receiving it. I developed this eerie stare that would literally bring the girls I dated to tears. The odd thing was, they would ask me to do it, get scared, and then ask me to stop. This behavior was repeated over and over. It was a scary game to them. But for me, it was more than a game.

I would stand in the shower and try to conjure demonic power. I would stare at the showerhead in hopes of moving it with my mind. I am telling you today that it moved, it really moved. At times it scared me, but I could not deny my craving for the power. I wanted to be connected to something greater than myself.

Each one of us longs to worship something. We long to be fulfilled and to have power. Without Christ, we long to be important and to have people notice us. When I told people in my circle what I was doing, they were thrilled. They wanted to conduct a séance and have me lead it. Although I was afraid, I would do it for the rush of power. Praise God, the timing never worked out.

When I accepted Jesus Christ into my life, I shared this story with my Godmother, Sylvia Rogers. She had me confess this to my pastor, who then prayed over me and rebuked the ties and strongholds that had developed in my life through attraction to the Satanic Church. Hallelujah and amen. If you think this is not happening in the world today, think again. Groups openly sing about and display in their videos the devil, voodoo, and cultlike behavior. I challenge you to visit your local bookstore and check out the religion section. In it, you will find The Satanic Bible and other cult books. Stand there and you'll see young people reading it flippantly, as they would the newspaper.

Where do they get such ideas? In their music. It is played at the mall, at the dentist's office, in the car, at sporting events, during commercials, and even in public schools. That's right, public schools. My school rewarded good behavior with being able to play devil rock music in class for everyone. I have worked in the school system as an adult, and the teachers are still doing it.

While I was recently working in a junior high school, I saw the female physical education teacher reward her students by playing some of the filthiest, perverse, sex rap that I had ever heard. How was she playing it? On the brand new, state-of-the-art sound system that the school had purchased. Ever wonder how those tax dollars are being spent?

To top it off, there are after school programs across the nation drawing kids in to keep them off the streets. They provide a big screen TV to watch pathetic MTV, and a sound system to play the devil's music. It's hard for me to believe that this is a better alternative. Not to mention the "Christian" teen centers that are playing the same garbage.

It is time for parents to wake up and take responsibility for their children. You are not being intrusive if you go through your children's music collection. In fact, you had better. Don't listen to the lies of the world that include, "it is just a phase they are going through." If you care, get involved now, before the situation worsens. I am telling you from personal experience and research, you will be sorry if you don't.

"Lest Satan should take advantage of us; for we are not ignorant of his devices."
2 Corinthians 2:11

Chapter 12

IN THE NET

"Dizzy, drunk and fightin'
On tequila white lightnin'
My glass is getting shorter
On whiskey, ice and water
So come on and have a good time
And get blinded out of your mind
So don't worry about tomorrow
Take it today
Forget about the cheque
We'll get hell to pay
Have a drink on me."
"Have a Drink On Me" by AC/DC
(http://www.purelyrics.com/index.php?lyrics=pmtdcesy)

    I was sleepy and my eyes were nearly closed. My hair had received the normal morning "once-over." My clothes matched, although Levi's and an Ozzy Osbourne t-shirt weren't hard to match. I hated to wake up early even back then, but it was showtime. I was in a band, and today was something special. I was joining my drunken, rock 'n' roll addicted friends in our Senior Variety Show. We were all set to appear as the band AC/DC and play the song "You Shook Me All Night Long."
    John, Roy, Greg and I sat in the school parking lot sipping tequila. We had all been to concerts and knew how to perform the act. If we were going to be like our "heroes," we would need to get drunk, get crazy, and sing about sex. So we were busy with the first requirement and planning out the rest.
    Greg slipped out of the car first. He was always the one afraid we would get caught. Roy went right behind him, as those two were never separated. Never. John and I kicked back in the seat and smiled. We both liked to drink, and having those two leave left more for us. John and I were playing the part of brothers Angus and Malcolm Young (guitarists for AC/DC) that day. It was fitting for us, as we were well on our way to becoming brothers of the bottle. (I am pleased to report at the time of this book's printing that John is now following God.) Finally the bell rang, and we strolled into school. We

agreed to get hall passes immediately and meet later to plan out the stage show. We were playing two shows that day — the first for the junior high and the second for the high school. This would require two trips to the parking lot to ingest our "liquid courage." We were not concerned, as we had more then ample supplies.

Within minutes, John and I met and headed to the auditorium. The stage was being set up. We would be the second band in the show. No problem. I thought back to the day when I was in junior high and a group of five senior high schoolers played the song "Heavy Metal" by Sammy Hagar. I fell in love with the rock and roll world that day. Those five guys shined in the spotlight and I had it set in my heart to do the same this day.

John played Angus. I played Malcolm. Angus, in real life, dances and spins and displays incredible energy throughout the night. Malcolm, to the best of my knowledge, stands in one spot and plays guitar. John and I decided that we would split the antics between us. John would walk around stage banging his head the entire time, and I would play the solo while spinning around on the floor. The plan was complete.

The first band played and the crowd went crazy. We could barely hear each other talk backstage. I was getting goose bumps, butterflies were stirring in my stomach, and the liquid courage was reaching peak sensation. The stage went black, the crowd grew silent, and the MC announced, "Now presenting — Insane Warrior." We were on.

Within seconds, you could hear a group of young kids screaming at the top of their lungs. The euphoria was building. John was banging his head, Roy was strutting with his bass guitar, Greg was lip-syncing the lyrics, Matt was slapping the skins, and I was preparing for my solo. Now donning camouflage pants, the Ozzy shirt, Magic Johnson brand shoes and two dangling skeleton earrings, I was dressed for success. Then came my solo.

Everyone backed up and made room. I slid down on the floor and began to run in circles while lying on my side. I then arched my back, placed my weight on my neck, and performed in a way that would truly be embarrassing for a boy's mother to see.

The crowd was going completely nuts and I wasn't far behind. I knew they liked what they saw and I felt that we were about to secure my wish of out-performing those guys from the Senior Variety Show of the past. I jumped up and we finished the song. Then we gathered together to take a bow to express our appreciation for the enthusiasm these young ones had displayed.

One show down and another to go. Back to the parking lot. Back to the tequila. Back to the head-banging, and back to spinning on the floor. The music played. The crowd screamed. I had become "hooked" in junior high, but now I was "in the net."

"And that they may come to their senses and escape the snare of the devil, having been taken captive by him to do his will."
2 Timothy 2:26

Chapter 13

THE COUGH

> "My life was empty
> Forever on a down
> Until you took me,
> Showed me around
> My life is free now,
> My life is clear
> I love you sweet leaf,
> Though you can't hear . . .
> C'mon let's go,
> Alright
> Try it out! . . .
> Won't ya try the Sweet Leaf?
> Oh yeah! . . .
> Hey! Keep on smokin' it! . . ."
>
> "Sweet Leaf" by Ozzy Osbourne
> (http://geocities.com/Heartland/Bluffs/8924/ozzmancometh.html)

No way. I would never ever smoke pot. Others were smoking it and I condemned them. I would not date anyone that smoked it. Not a chance. But then I heard a cough. "Uhughh, uhughh, uhughh, uhughh" blared on the stereo. It was the sound of a man coughing. It was implying that he was coughing from trying to hold the marijuana smoke in his lungs to get high. Ozzy was my god. His music was my gospel. The song lyrics rang out, "the world will love you sweet leaf." Over and over I listened. When we watched him live in concert, Ozzy screamed, "Keep on smokin' it." Hooked by the music, I finally gave in.

My friends Tim, Steve and Mel rolled up. "Plont, we've got some smoke. C'mon, Ozzy, 'keep on smokin' it.' " I was at a party with Rusty, and of course Bonnie. I said to her, "I'll be back. C'mon boys, let's go. Alright, try it out!" Minutes later, the rolling paper was lit, the smell emanated, and I inhaled the "sweet leaf" deep into my lungs. In moments, I was high. Power. Invincibility. Rage. Blackouts. Paranoia. These accompanied the rush.

It was the first time I had ingested the "sweet leaf," but it would not my last. Unfortunately, it became more and more available, and I became more and more willing. It was not the fact that I liked it, but rather that I enjoyed the image it portrayed. I wanted to be a rock star and all the rock stars I knew of endorsed it.

It should come as no surprise that satan pushes drugs in his music, yet many do not believe that drug use is addressed in the Bible. Contrary to what those who smoke pot and feel it is a blessed herb of the Lord think, the Bible condemns its use. If one goes back and studies the Greek language, they will find the word "pharmakia." In modern translation, it is often written as "sorcery." It primarily signified "the use of drugs." God makes a point to talk about what happens to those who "use drugs" without repentance. It says in His word in Revelation 22:15 they will "not inherit the kingdom of God" (cross-reference Revelation 9:20 and Galatians 5:21). It goes on to say in Revelation 21:8, they will "have their part in the lake which burns with fire and brimstone," which is quite the opposite of the liberal view of "smoke up with the approval of God."

It is also interesting to note *Vine's Dictionary* for the word "sorcery." It states: "In 'sorcery,' the use of drugs, whether simple or potent, was generally accompanied by incantations and appeals to occult powers, with the provision of various charms, amulets, etc., professedly designed to keep the applicant or patient from the attention and power of demons." Well, let us now dissect those words. The following are definitions from *Webster's New World Dictionary of the American Language.* Incantations — "to sing, chant." Charm — "song," "originally, a chanted word, phrase, or verse assumed to have magic power to help or hurt." Amulet — "something worn, often around the neck, as a protection against injury or evil; a charm."

What do popular music concerts offer? Drugs, songs, chants, appeals to occult activity. Need I say more? Once again, God is clear in what He does not want to happen on earth. And He most certainly does not want His "children" participating in these activities. We have already talked in previous chapters about the power of music. We have talked about its link to the occult. Now we are talking about the fact that it pushes drug use.

Believe me, Ozzy Osbourne is not the only one preaching to "keep on smokin' it."

Why did I quit "smokin' it"? Maybe it was the blackouts. Maybe it was the paranoia. Maybe it was the fact that I could not control my anger and physically assaulted my best friend, not once, but twice. Maybe it was the "tunnel" vision that lasted for hours. Maybe it was the fact I could feel a demonic presence whenever I smoked it. Maybe it was the foreshadowed flames that God allowed me to feel. Whatever it was, I knew inside it was wrong, and I didn't need anyone to tell me.

"But the . . . sorcerers . . . shall have their part in the lake which burns with fire and brimstone, which is the second death."
Revelation 21:8

Chapter 14

HEZEKIAH BEN AARON

I present to you another witness who will testify to the truth of the devil's involvement. His name is Hezekiah Ben Aaron.

Ben Aaron was interviewed in 1985 by a newspaper called *New Solidarity*. At that time, he was the third-ranking member of the Church of Satan. Ben Aaron claimed that his church had started bands such as Blue Oyster Cult, The Who, Black Sabbath and Ozzy Osbourne, as well as others. The leader of the Church of Satan was Anton LaVey, although he reportedly was only a front man for the true leader, Kenneth Anger. Anger was the man who had earlier turned the Rolling Stones on to the occult. [1]

The following quotes are excerpts from the Ben Aaron interview:

> I was working for the church . . . The church had other people who were middlemen for other companies. There were middlemen for Apple (set up by the Beatles), Warner Brothers, and other record companies. Someone would come to me and say, "I have a tape recording, and I'd like for you to check it out." A few days later, Ben Aaron would call back and set up another meeting that would be secretly recorded. He continues: "I'd hand you $100,000, and you wouldn't sign anything. What you wouldn't know is that a mirror on the back of the wall is a one-way mirror and we're tape recording and photographing, or video taping everything that goes on. The payback, if you fail to make the group work, is really bad. Sometimes it's up to 60 percent on the dollar." [2] Ben Aaron continued by saying, "We send you to a store, we provide you with uniforms, and we provide you with amplifiers. It's all paid through the money we gave you. We set you up with a road tour. We set you up with engagements. We book you." [3]

"Modern electronic rock music, born in the early '60s, has always been influenced by Satanic cults," writes author Donald Phau. "The Satanists control the major rock groups through drugs, sex, threats of violence, and even murder." (4) If that does not send a chill down your spine, then you had better check for a heartbeat. By the way, today Ben Aaron is a devout Christian.

1. Donald Phau, "The Satanic Roots of Rock," http://www.av1611.org/othpubls/roots.html, 14.
2. Ibid.
3. Ibid.
4. Phau, "The Satanic Roots of Rock,"1.

Chapter 15

THE FIELD

> "No stop signs, no speed limits
> Nobody's gonna slow me down
> Like a wheel, gonna spin it
> Nobody's gonna mess me 'round
> Hey Satan, paid my dues
> Playing in a rocking band
> Hey Momma — look at me
> I'm on the way to the promised land
> I'm on the highway to hell
> Don't stop me . . . "
>
> "Highway to Hell" by AC/DC
> (http://www.highwaytoacdc.com)

St. Francis Catholic School was coming to town. They had beaten us in football for the last 20 years straight and we despised them. They were Catholic "religious" boys, and we believed the only reason they beat us was that they had God on their side.

This year would provide no great hope of breaking the endless chain of agonizing defeats, so we would settle the issue off the field. Rudy, Geoff, Skyler (my close friends) and I were going to give them something to remember. I was hopelessly in love with Bonnie, and of course she went along for the ride. I held the title of her "other boyfriend," and would do nearly anything to obtain first place.

I had been analyzing *The Satanic Bible* by Anton LaVey and had shared it with the crew. We agreed to conduct a satanic séance soon, but this night we would pull off another surprise. Undoubtedly, St. Francis would take US 31 to our high school, and there was one perfect hill for the event. We brought cans of white spray paint and began to use both lanes of "31" as our canvas. In eight-foot-high letters we inscribed "Satan Kills St. Francis." The rush of this secret pact and the demonic confidence I displayed attracted Bonnie. She was enticed by the whole "satan" thing. Next, we decided to hang a bloody mannequin donning a St. Francis jersey in front of our school. We searched high and low, but thank God the five of us could not find one.

On game night, we arrived two hours early. Out came the clown make-up. A minimum of 15 players became novice artists as we inscribed upside down crosses, the numbers "666," and satanic pentagrams on our faces. Next, we hit the gym. Every home game had the "black room." The "black room" consisted of 30 young men gathered in one end of our high basketball court. The gym darkness was pierced only by a small red and white exit sign. You couldn't even see your hand in front of your face. Metallica screamed louder then if they were appearing live. Some of us sat and rocked back and forth. Others slammed into and punched walls. Others just paced and cussed. I tried to develop the demonic powers I believed I harbored in an attempt to steal away my fear of running down that field. Our coaches never stepped into that gym — it was the devil's sanctuary, and we believed it to be ours.

Then came our call to the field. We assembled and entered. The St. Catholic players looked on in disbelief, as I am sure to them it was a joke. Then came the words, "Hey Plont, it's mother's night, you know." Fear traveled down my backbone. To describe my mother with one word, it's "pure." She is the type of lady who convicts you of sin with a glance. She was the person for whom I held the highest esteem. When she walked on that field, she stepped on the devil's head.

I will always remember how I turned and gave her a flower (a ritual on mother's night) as I removed my helmet. And I will never forget the look on her face as she saw mine. She just quietly said, "What are you doing?" I smiled without answering and faced the crowd instead. The black make-up mixed with tears pooled above my lips as I stood there ashamed. My days of being on that satanic majestic mountain were gone with a stare.

> **"When pride comes, then comes shame;
> But with the humble is wisdom."**
>
> **Proverbs 11:2**

Chapter 16

ANTON LAVEY

The fifth and final person in this group that we are going to talk about is the former leader of the Church of Satan and the writer of *The Satanic Bible,* Anton LaVey, who is now also deceased.

"Anton Szandor LaVey (1930-1997), like Charles Manson, Timothy Leary, and other messianic pop gurus, was a notorious figure of the 1960s subculture of the social experiment." He served as the high priest for the Church of Satan and is the professed author of *The Satanic Bible.* One-third of *The Satanic Bible* was taken directly from one of Aleister Crowley's writings called *The Equinox.* Proper attribution was not given to Crowley by LaVey. [1]

No one described the essence of the free love '60s better than LaVey and the Church of Satan. LaVey admitted that Satanism is simply a worshiping of one's self when he stated: "This is a very selfish religion. We believe in greed, we believe in selfishness, we believe in all the lustful thoughts that motivate man, because this is man's natural, uh, feeling." [2]

The following are verses from *The Satanic Bible*:

> Free love, in the Satanic concept, means exactly that — freedom to either be faithful to one person or to indulge your sexual desires with as many others as you feel is necessary to satisfy particular needs. [3]

> Therefore, the most simplified description of the Satanic belief is: Indulgence instead of abstinence. [4]

In a later printing of *The Satanic Bible,* LaVey's biographer, Burton H. Wolfe, wrote in the introduction: "Repressed people have burst their bonds. Sex has exploded. The collective libido has been released, in movies and literature, on the streets and in the home. People are dancing topless and bottomless . . . There is a ceaseless universal quest for entertainment, gourmet foods and wines, enjoyment of the here and now . . . There is a mood of neopaganism and hedonism, and from it there have emerged a wide variety of brilliant individuals, doctors, lawyers, teachers, engineers, teachers, writers, stockbrokers, real estate developers, actors and actresses, mass communication media people (to cite a few categories of Satanists) who are interested in formalizing and perpetuating this all-pervading religion (satanism) and way of life." (5)

Well, there you have it. These are the men who set the stage for today's world of popular music and all of its negative influences. Each one of them is intricately linked. They are evil men carrying out an evil plan. Regrettably so, over the next few chapters we are going to look at how these men have become incredibly successful in obtaining their goals.

As I close this chapter, consider this word for word (uh's included) quote from occult writer Robert Anton Wilson before Aleister Crowley's death. He "sparked a worldwide revival of paganism . . . Well, in 1918, Crowley, uh, took the great magical oath, which was a serious thing to, uh, Crowley, uh, and he took an oath that he would surrender all of his magical powers that he had achieved until that date to concentrate his energies, single-pointedly, on the one task of, uh, destroying Christianity and, uh, reviving, uh, paganism. And I think, if you look around the world, it's pretty obvious that Crowley has been, uh, a remarkable success. Paganism has made a big comeback, in an organized way. Neopagan groups, in an unorganized way, our whole society has become more pagan." (6)

1 John 2:16 states: "Do not love the world or the things in the world. If anyone loves the world, the love of the Father is not in him. For all that is in the world -- the lust of the flesh, the lust of the eyes, and the pride of life, is not of the Father but is of the world." (7) Those are the same things that satan promised to Eve in the garden and to every man today. Just do your own thing. Some people would say, "Michael, I don't love the world or the things in it!" Well, let us go one step further to James 4:4. It reads " . . . Do you not know that friendship with

the world is enmity with God? Whoever therefore wants to be a friend of the world makes himself an enemy of God." [8]

It is our choice to be a friend of God or an enemy of God. Some people say, "I only listen to a little bit of it, it only influences me a little!" Therefore, they are only a little enemy of God. Richard Pellegrino, who is a medical doctor and consultant to the entertainment industry, states that music produces endorphin highs, sometimes even subconsciously. "Take it from a brain guy. In 25 years of working with the brain, I still cannot affect a person's mind the way that one simple song can." [9]

To continue, 1 John 2:17 states: "And the world is passing away, and the lust of it; but he who does the will of God abides forever." [10] We can follow our own will and pay the consequences as Eve did, or we can follow the will of God and abide with Him forever on earth and in heaven.

1. Zeena LaVey and Nikolas Schrek, "Anton LaVey: Legend and Reality," February 2, 1998, (http://fcos.us/aslv.html)
2. Eric Holmberg, *Hell's Bells 2: The Dangers of Rock 'n' Roll*, 2001, Reel 2 Real Ministries, video.
3. Anton LaVey, *The Satanic Bible*, (New York, NY: Avon, 1976), 66.
4. LaVey, *The Satanic Bible*, 81.
5. Burton Wolfe, 1969, Introduction to *The Satanic Bible*.
6. Holmberg, *Hell's Bells 2*, video.
7. Max Lucado, *The Inspirational Study Bible: New King James Version of the Bible*, (Dallas, Tx: Thomas Nelson, Inc., 1982.)
8. Ibid.
9. Holmberg, *Hell's Bells 2*, video.
10. Lucado, *New King James Version of the Bible*.

Chapter 17

STUNTED GROWTH

> "OPP, How Can I Explain It
> O Is For Other, P Is For People Scratchin' Temple,
> The Last P . . . Well . . . It's Not That Simple
> It's Sorta Like Another Way To Call A Cat A Kitten . . .
> As For The Ladies, OPP Means Something Gifted
> The First Two Letters Are The Same But The Last Is Something Different
> It's The Longest, Loveliest, Lean — I Call It The Leanest
> It's Another Five Letter Word Rhymin' With Cleanest And Meanest."
>
> "O.P.P." by Naughty By Nature
> (http://www.purelyrics.com/index.php?lyrics=saqzedhq)

I remember the first time I saw the video. Guys and girls alike singing and smiling and claiming their shame. They had done more to promote immorality in one song than most groups could do throughout their careers. To me, it was a mission statement.

Why do I need to have a girlfriend when I can I easily date someone else's? Why should I have to commit to a relationship when I can be the second man? I believed there were great benefits to adopting this program. I had the thrill of getting away with something. I never had to spend a penny on the girls. I got to walk past their boyfriends and chuckle to myself. It was all about me. I had the power.

There was Walt and his Katrina. Nate and Bonnie. Carl and Lori. Krista and Benji. Matty and Rob. They were all in long-term relationships. They trusted each other. Each time she cheated, his heart was ripped out. Each time, I was involved.

One could read this and think I am bragging about conquests and victories, but rather it is the opposite. I am simply stating a fact. What I chose to do was wrong. What they chose to do was wrong. But each one of us were establishing a pattern in our lives. We were learning that in relationships, it's okay to lie, it's okay to deceive, and it's okay to choose one hour of lust over a lifetime of devotion.

Quite plausibly you could say, "Mike, negative influences are in more then just music. It's also portrayed in television shows and movies." I will, hands down, answer, "You are right." Yet the majority of the time, what is playing in the background as betrayal is taking place? Popular music.

Those tricks and schemes I cultivated as a teenager only blossomed as I became a young adult. I continued, as stated later in this book, the role of "home wrecker" until the I met Jesus. Then the chains were finally broken. Sad, but true, many of my now 30-something teenage friends are continuing in the same lifestyles. Our generation was spoon-fed adultery, like the 1960s fed the free love theory. Is in any wonder that the divorce rate is so high? It is any wonder that adultery takes place inside and outside the church? It is any wonder that we have a generation of uncommitted people?

It is not a coincidence. The '80s generation was spoon-fed an anti-God buffet, and I guarantee it is happening again, right now, to your children who are listening to popular music. If you take a look at the people who are committing adultery today, you will find one underlying fact: "stunted growth." It is my belief that people in the world are suffering because of the stunted growth they experienced in their teen years. This is when they made choices to consume alcohol, become promiscuous, and use illegal drugs. Is it any wonder they made those choices with the musical influences they were ingesting? This book is poignant in pointing out that influence.

Everyone reading this book can now look at their friends from high school who have not changed since they walked out those doors. They were smoking pot then and they are now. They were drunks then and they are now. They were unfaithful in relationships then and they are now. They were listening to low-rate, garbage-infested, mind-warping music and they are now. This is no coincidence.

Donald Phau was right when he said that it was a demonic plan to get young people hooked on this music in the '60s and '70s and then assimilate them into places of leadership. That is why we have judges busted for smoking pot at rock and roll concerts. That is why we have teachers having sex with their students. That is why we have teachers selling drugs to their students. That is why we had a president who could not stop himself from habitually committing adultery while he was supposed to be running our country. "Do what thou wilt" is running rampant. These are some of the most powerful, influential people in America, and yet they suffer from "stunted growth."

"For a man is a slave to whatever has mastered him."
2 Peter 2:19b

Chapter 18

JEFF FENHOLT

A man by the name of Jeff Fenholt has written a tell-all book about his life. He is the former lead singer for the group Black Sabbath, and also, ironically, starred in the Broadway show *Jesus Christ Superstar*, which has sold over 15 million double albums. Fenholt, at one time, was deeply involved in the occult. On one occasion he flipped out and nearly beat his wife to death. Another time, he actually beat his daughter's dog to death. He had this to say about the link between the rock music world and the devil:

> Reeni (his wife) began noticing that I was getting deeper and deeper into drugs and more and more involved in the occult. I was going to parties with Satanists and hanging out with people who conjured demons. Many people will still challenge the fact that there is Satanism in the heavy rock scene. I'm here to tell you that Satanism runs long, hard and deep and is the basic undergirding of all rock music. Many successful musicians, rock groups, management organizations that I encountered were involved in Satanism, the occult or the so-called New Age Movement. This is not a coincidence! [1,2]

Fenholt finishes his quote by explaining that in Matthew 16:15-18 Jesus said, "Upon this rock I will build My church." Just prior to this, Jesus had asked his disciples who they believed He was. The apostle Peter answered, "You are the Christ, the Son of the living God." Peter had confessed his faith in Jesus. Jesus called that faith a "rock," and then stated He would build His church upon that faith. Fenholt goes on. "Having been in the occult and knowing the devil as I did, I believe that Satan has a counterfeit for everything. I believe that somewhere in hell, Satan held a meeting with his demons and made the statement: 'Upon this rock (referring to music), I will build my church.'" [3]

1. Jeff Fenholt, *From Darkness to Light* (Tulsa, Oklahoma: Harrison House, 1994), 58.
2. Fenholt, *From Darkness to Light*, 44.
3. Fenholt, *From Darkness to Light*, 45.

Chapter 19

VILE WORSHIP

> "I've listened to preachers
> I've listened to fools
> I've watched all the dropouts
> Who make their own rules
> One person conditioned
> To rule and control
> The media sells it and you live the role
> Mental wounds not healing
> Who and what's to blame?
> I'm going off the rails on a crazy train."
>
> "Crazy Train" by Ozzy Osbourne
> (http://www.geocities.com/Heartland/Bluffs/8924/tribute.html)

As I piled into the van that morning, little did I know how the next few days' events would change my life. I was headed to my first concert. Not surprisingly, it was an Ozzy Osbourne concert. It was the normal crew of Mac, Tim, Sammy and me, and then a few others who were along for the ride. We left early that day as the concert was a four-and-a-half hour drive away. We stopped an hour from the concert venue at one of Tim's old stomping grounds to buy some "mind-altering, left-handed non-filters" (better known as weed). It was a given. Weed, Ozzy concert. Ozzy concert, weed. They simply went together. We bought it, smoked it, and shared it that day. Ozzy was a god, the god of rock and roll, and we were going to worship him.

We arrived at Joe Louis Arena in Detroit at 7:00 p.m. Security guards were searching the car next to ours in the parking garage. They found weed, confiscated it, and told the kids to beat it. Then security came to our car. "You got any weed?" "No, sir," we answered. They stared at us intently and then walked up to our vehicle. The security guard looked Tim straight in the eye and whispered, "Do you want to buy any?" We stood in the middle of a urine-drenched parking lot in disbelief. With half-naked girls everywhere, music blaring at 100 decibels, and being drunk half out of my mind, I thought this was heaven.

As we entered the arena, it was total chaos. The police were in the forefront. Everyone was searched. Everyone and everywhere. The guy in front of me had hits of acid, and he kissed the cement wall faster than I had ever seen a man do so in my life. The officer flung that boy like he was Superman, and he stuck like Spiderman. "Are you with him, boy?" "No, Sir," I said. Mac hollered, "liar," and before I knew it, I was Spiderman. Tim vouched for me, and minutes later we were in our seats.

The warm-up band was made up of some young guys who called themselves "Metallica." They played four songs and then cussed out the audience for crowding the stage. Metallica requested several times that people back up, but it was to no avail. We cheered, "Ozzy, Ozzy" to their objections. They cussed us out again, said we were pathetic, and then left.

Thirty minutes later came the darkness. Eighteen thousand people in a room with no lights on. Pitch black. Then the music. The eeriest music you'll ever hear. I called it "church music," as I did not know what church music sounded like. It got louder and louder and louder. Every hair on my body stood up. I began to rock back and forth. We began to chant, "Ozzy, Ozzy, Ozzy." Something spiritual was happening to me and it thrilled me. Then a light, a small light on the stage with a man standing in it. He raised his hands in the air, and not 17,999, but all 18,000 people raised their hands. I had tears running down my face now, and the words that came from my lips were, "I love you, Ozzy." The music was at its loudest, the fear was at its greatest, and the man in the light said, "Let the madness begin." And it did.

For the next two hours we would sing, dance, cheer, smoke dope, watch people have sex, and listen to Osbourne tell us we were "going to hell" and we were going to have a "good ol' time down there." We did everything he commanded, including going crazy to the point of people fighting with the police and being arrested. I was scared to death, but something kept drawing me in. It was as if something entered me and made me feel like someone else. I no longer felt my pain or my foolish fears; I felt invincible. I literally felt the presence of the devil. I loved it, yet it scared me. I woke up to a hangover, an empty wallet, a shameful heart, and of course, "the eyes." This would not be the last time.

Over the next nine years, I would see Ozzy five more times, and each time, his concerts got worse. We would take young women with us who would ride down to the concert in a "normal" state and they would return home with us drunk and half-naked. Those concerts changed people — it was like a trance. You were no longer a fan, you had become a convert.

The last concert I watched live was in 1996, one year before I was saved. Ozzy's act had become more extreme. The same opening, the same naked girls, the same dope, the same cussing, but this time he had his son with him, an innocent little boy. Ozzy hollered, "I want my son to know what a woman looks like." Immediately, a woman near the stage began to disrobe. Osbourne then peeled his screaming, crying, little boy off his leg and forced him to look at the naked woman as the child screamed, "Daddy, no!" It sent chills down my spine. I wanted to puke. What had I become?

I headed for the exit. On my way out, I tried to bum money from my friend to buy an Ozzy hockey jersey (that bore the number 666). Thank God he wouldn't let me. As we walked out the last gate, I heard Ozzy say, "We're all headed to hell, but we're gonna to have a good ol' time down there." Deep in my heart I thought, "Man, I hope not."

"They (Belshazzar and his lords) drank wine and praised the gods of gold and silver, bronze and iron, wood and stone. . . That very night Belshazzar, king of the Chaldeans, was slain."

Daniel 5:4, 30

Chapter 20

THE POWER OF MUSIC

What does the Bible say about the power of music? The first book of Samuel 16:23 (King James Version) reads, "And so it was, whenever the distressing spirit sent from God was upon Saul, that David would take a harp and play it with his hand. Then Saul would become refreshed as well, and the distressing spirit would depart from him." Matthew Henry, in his concise commentary, declares the following regarding this passage:

> If God and His grace do not rule us, sin and Satan will have possession of us. It is a pity that music, which may be serviceable to the good temper of the mind, should ever be abused, to support vanity and luxury, and made an occasion of drawing the heart from God and serious things. [1]

In 1952, a disk jockey in Cleveland, Ohio, by the name of Alan Freed, coined the term "rock and roll" while describing some new music on his afternoon radio show. He borrowed the term from the juke joints of the South. The term "rock and roll" meant to fornicate. Suddenly, a new music genre was born. Freed soon moved to one of the world's largest stations — located in New York City — to do his show. Seven years later, Freed tearfully resigned amidst a scandal for taking kickbacks to play the music of certain groups. In another five years, Freed died drunk and broke at the age of 42. "The man who named an era was its first victim." [2]

Cultural critic Michael Ventura states:

> . . . rock 'n' roll was a term from the juke joints of the South when a music was being heard that had no name . . . In those juke joints, rock 'n' roll hadn't meant the name of music, it meant to f---. When, finally in the mid-'50s, the songs started being played by white people and aired on the radio — "Rock Around the Clock," "Good Rockin'

Tonight," "Reelin' and Rockin' " — the meaning hadn't changed. [3]

Can music influence the human body and mind? Nearly every function of the human body is moved by music. Research shows it affects "digestion, internal secretions, circulation, nutrition, respiration," neural networks of the brain,[4] and one's major internal organs. Our bodies not only hear music, but we feel it. Many people today claim they no longer pay attention to the words, they simply like the way it feels. [5]

At a recent Christian conference on aggression, Pastor Bill Gothard taught:

> The frantic, almost uncontrollable energy level released at a typical rock concert is often mistaken by the audience and the performers alike as a demonstration of musical artistic ability. Whether they know it or not, the primary power and draw of this style of music is their ability to "turn on" the listener by triggering their "fight or flight" (adrenaline reaction) syndrome.

The article went on to say that once the syndrome is triggered, the body actually gets high off its own internal drug. This has been found to lead to increased awareness and energy, and also a tendency towards antisocial behavior. [6]

Ventura, the same researcher who told us where the name rock and roll came from, gave us the following statement:

> Music research has done a masterful job of tracing modern rock music back to its sources in voodoo worship. It explains how the goal of the music is to have the gods of sensuality connect with the performers and the listeners and infuse a supernatural power to enjoy the pleasures of the flesh. [7]

We have now affirmed a history of the "do what thou wilt" attitude promoted by Aleister Crowley.

In a study on the neurophysiology of rhythm, two researchers confirmed "our basic claim is that rock music itself induces a behavioral link between aggression and sexuality." (8)

Dr. Paul King, medical director of the adolescent unit of Charter Lakeside Hospital in Memphis, Tennessee, stated that "drug use, hate, devil worship, mutilation, brutality and suicide are buzz words in today's rock music." King conducted a study of his 470 patients and they informed him that he would have to listen to their music to understand them. So he did. (9)

After listening and reinterviewing them, he concluded, "They said music was a very important influence in their lives. In fact, it was their religion. The use of drugs and alcohol had erased any concept of God that these kids had, and it got replaced with this new religion . . . music." (10)

Joseph Crow, a researcher from the University of Seattle, also studied rock music. He found the following results: "Rock is a use of music based on mathematical formulae to condition the mind through calculated frequencies (vibrations), and it is used to modify the body chemistry to make the mind susceptible to modification and indoctrination. Rock music can be (and is) employed for mind bending, reeducation, and reorganization." (11) He went on to say what we are fighting against is "not just a mind-controlling cult, a powerful addiction, or a false religion, but all three at the same time. Any one of these would be a challenge. All three together are a stronghold of disastrous dimensions." (12)

As a Christian, I cannot deny the power of music. Time and time again, I have seen the lives of men and women changed during music services. I, myself, gave my heart to Christ in the middle of a song service. I have seen countless others saved, delivered, convicted and healed during song service. God releases the power of His Spirit and anoints the music to tug at our souls.

But there also is a power in rock music. It is simply anointed by the devil. As we discussed earlier, in citing Ezekiel 28:13, Lucifer (satan) was directly connected to the music services in heaven. His job, or at least the one that he has assumed, is to draw man away from God, and why wouldn't he choose to use something at which he is skilled? Why wouldn't he use music? I believe the answer is that he can and he does.

Let's stop, just for a second, and hear what these men say about the power of music.

> William Shakespeare stated, "Music oft hath such a charm to make good bad . . ." (13)

> In his book *The Closing of the American Mind*, Dr. Alan Bloom wrote, "Music is the soul's primitive and primary speech . . . Armed with music, man can damn rational doubt. Out of music emerge the gods that suit it, and they educate men by their example and their commandments." (14)

> David Elkind, in his book *The Hurried Child* stated, "One of the most underestimated influences in the world today is the music industry." (15)

> Vladimir Lenin, the cofounder of Communism, once stated, " One quick way to destroy society is through its music." (16)

> Perhaps no quote on the power of music is more eye-opening than one by Eddie Manson, Oscar winner and one-time president of the American Society of Musical Arrangers: "Music is used everywhere to condition the human mind. It can be just as powerful as a drug and much more dangerous, because nobody takes musical manipulation very seriously." (17)

There is little doubt that music has power over people today, as it is a huge part of their lives. They wake up to it, play to it, work to it, and fall asleep to it. It is in commercials, stores, offices, sporting events, etc. Many of today's youth claim they do not listen to the words, they merely like the beat. But as we have seen, music influences the mind differently. That is why advertisers use catchy tunes for their products. Almost everyone knows the jingles, "Like a good neighbor, State Farm is there," or " Oscar Meyer has a way with B-O-L-O-G-N-A." Theme songs from television programs like *The Flintstones* or *The Brady Bunch* are also filed away in the human mind. Although they may be harmless, they demonstrate one's ability to retain music easily. That can be dangerous. [18]

If you have even a remote interest in professional sports, you realize that rock and roll music is played during most breaks in play. Some of the most offensive music released is played at these events, with none worse than the song "Hell's Bells" sung by the rock band AC/DC. The following is brief look at the lyrics:

> "I'm a rolling thunder, a pouring rain
> I'm comin' on like a hurricane
> My lightning's flashing across the sky
> You're only young but you're gonna die
> I won't take no prisoners, won't spare no lives
> Nobody's putting up a fight
> I got my bell, I'm gonna take you to hell
> I'm gonna get you, Satan get you
> Hell's Bells, yeah Hell's Bells, you got me ringing Hell's Bells." [19]

Another popular song that is played is "Who Let the Dogs Out?" by the Baha Men. Glance at those lyrics. They are not talking about someone leaving the back door of the house open, but rather a man and woman engaged in a particular sex act.

And how about commercials? One of the biggest offenders is the auto industry. We have ads for Dodge trucks playing the song "Just Push Play," which repeatedly uses the f-word and makes references to drug use and sex with an underage girl. Cadillac is using the song "Rock and Roll" by Led Zeppelin. That song is about having sexual intercourse, and let us remember the groups' close ties to Satanic, baby-murdering Aleister Crowley. Also, do not forget Ford, which just recently began to use the Rolling Stones song "Start Me Up," which has obvious sexual overtones.

In Proverbs 4:20, God states that there are two primary doorways to the heart — the eyes and ears. It reads, "My son, pay attention to what I say; listen closely to my words. Do not let them out of your sight, keep them within your heart." (New International Version [NIV]) This is to say that a great percentage of man's wisdom comes from what he sees and hears.

The Bible also differentiates between two types of wisdom, one of which originates with the devil. James 3:13-17 states, ". . . if you harbor bitter envy and selfish ambition in your hearts, do not boast about it or deny the truth. Such wisdom does not come down from heaven but is earthly, unspiritual, of the devil . . . But the wisdom that comes from heaven is first of all pure ..." (NIV) If man allows Satan to sow this "unspiritual" wisdom into his heart through the doorway of his eyes and ears, Galatians 6:8 states, "The one who sows to please his sinful nature, from that nature will reap destruction; . . ." (NIV) [20]

Now you might be saying, "Alright, hold the phone, Mike! I can admit there is power in music, and I can admit that the devil seeks to influence us and draw us away from God, but who is to say these artists and their music is drawn from the devil? Well let's hear from the artists and see what they say for themselves!

> Pete Townshend of the Who said, "When I'm on stage, I feel this incredible, almost spiritual experience ... when they occur, they are sacred." [21]

> Michael Jackson, who needs no introduction, stated, "On many an occasion when I'm dancing, I have felt touched by something sacred. In those moments, I felt my spirit soar, and become one with everything that exists." [22]

> John Anderson, lead singer for the band Yes says, "Music has always been religious. Music is a passion and a vehicle for understanding why we are here. It's a remembering of the past and ritual." [23]

"Otherwise I think of myself as kind of like as (sic) a holy roller preacher, I'm testifying, I'm getting everybody riled up for the power of almighty rock and roll," says Paul Stanley, lead singer of the rock band Kiss. (24)

The Beatles' frontman John Lennon said, "When the real music comes to me it has nothing to do with me, 'cause I'm just a channel. It's given to me and I transcribe it like a channel." (25)

Singer Alanis Morissette stated, "A lot of the songs were written in about 15 minutes to 45 minutes, just really quickly, . . . many times we felt as though it was being channeled through us." (26)

Dave "The Snake" Sabo of the rock band Skid Row: "Plus my song writing too, I'm very, very aware that when I write a good song I'm just acting as like (sic) a messenger, it comes from a higher source, you know, I'm not so egotistical that I think I have done this all on my own. I'm very, very aware there is a higher source sort of guiding me through this and I'm just acting as a messenger." (27)

Robert Palmer, lead vocalist of Led Zeppelin, in describing how their hit song "Stairway to Heaven" came to him: "I was holding a paper and pencil. Then all of a sudden, my hand was writing out words. 'There's a lady who's sure all that glitters is gold, and she's buying a stairway to heaven.' I just sat there and looked at the words and then I almost leapt out of my seat." (28)

Black Sabbath guitarist Tony Iommi stated, "We have always, within the band, said there is a fifth member, a mystical member, yeah." Drummer Bill Ward said, "We would literally show up in a room, and it was almost as if the songs were already written." He went on to say, "Although it is a rock and roll band, uh, there's a phenomenon involved where that stuff just comes from somewhere, and it just so happened that, that it, it, we, we happened to be the ones that it came to." [29]

Alternative singer Tori Amos said, "When people were asking me about the whole fairy thing, it was because I believe in the spirit side. I think music comes through dimensions. It's arrogant to think you can create music on your own, there's a cocreation going on. I don't know with whom, but there is this well that we all tap into . . ." She went on: "I feel like it's really kind of nice they come and use my body to say what they want to say. It's an energy force that comes and visits me." [30]

I remind you there is one true God. He has one adversary, and that adversary's name is Satan. God has not used these artists to channel His word. He has not stimulated their minds to provide these thoughts. And God has not used their bodies as some type of puppet or robot either. Their music does not glorify Him in the least bit, but these artists are telling us there is an outside force. If it is not the one true God, then it must be the former worship leader of heaven. (reread Ezekiel 28:13).

What about the performance itself — could it be perpetrated by demons?

Well known singer and guitarist Carlos Santana had this to say about his music: "It's a spiritual vibe, it's a spiritual hit, it's a hit you know, it's a hit that you can't get at church. I am the string, and the Supreme is the musician . . . It's like sometimes I'm not aware I can do some of these things on my guitar, because in reality, I'm not doing them. They are being done through me." [31]

Santana has been heralded across this world as a Christian. He is said to be a musician who has given his life over to God, and that God has blessed him with an incredible comeback on the music scene. Let's investigate this further.

During the 42nd annual Grammy Awards, Santana won nine Grammys, including Record of the Year, Album of the Year, and Song of the Year. He beat Michael Jackson's previous record of eight. Santana has a studio that he calls "church," where he has candles, "the word 'Metatron' spelled out in intricately painted picture letters on the floor, " and a yellow legal pad he uses to record the spiritual messages as they come to him, "like a fax machine." (32)

Santana told *Rolling Stone* that Metatron told him he was going to have a successful album and he would be bringing together a large group of entertainers to make it. Both came true. In the *Rolling Stone* article, Metatron is identified as the "eye inside the triangle." One particular man used the eye inside the triangle as the most significant symbol in his book called *The Book of the Law*. His name is Aleister Crowley. (33)

Santana goes on to say, "Metatron is the architect of physical life. Because of him, we can French-kiss, we can hug, we can get a hot dog, wiggle our toe. (34) Metatron wants something from me, and I know exactly what it is ... The people who listen to the music are connected to a higher form of themselves. That's why I get a lot of joy from this CD, because it's a personal invitation from me to people: Remember your divinity." (35)

Who does Santana believe is the leader of his music? Well let's take a look . . . Santana says, "You meditate and you got the candles, you got the incense and you've been chanting, and all of a sudden you hear this voice: 'Write this down' (36) The energy of devils and angels is the same energy; it's how you use it. It's fuel. There is a saying: If you scare all your devils away, the angels will go away with them. You know, the halo and the horns are the same thing. I mean it's okay to be spiritually horny — that's what creative genius is all about. Geniuses don't have time to think about how it's going to be received . . . they don't have time to think whether people like it or not, is it morally right, will God like it? I'm trying now, very graciously, to balance and validate angels and devils with the same reverence." (37)

Does not 2 Corinthians 6:14b state: "And what communion has light with darkness? Let me tell you, if you are a child of God, you do not need to validate angels and devils with the same reverence. [38] Also, one must consider the following bit of scripture (Deut 13:1-5) in reference to Santana's work.

> If there arises among you a prophet or dreamer of dreams, and he gives you a sign or wonder, and the sign or the wonder comes to pass, of which he spoke to you saying, "Let us go after other gods"— which you have not known — "and let us serve them," you shall not listen to the words of that prophet or that dreamer of dreams, for the Lord your God is testing you to know whether you love the Lord your God with all your heart and with all your soul. You shall walk after the Lord your God and fear Him, and keep His commandments and obey His voice; you shall serve Him and hold fast to Him. But that prophet or that dreamer of dreams shall be put to death, because he has spoken in order to turn you away from the Lord your God . . . So you shall put away the evil from your midst. [39]

If that is not enough proof, here are a few more quotes.

> Guitarist John McLaughlin: "One night we were playing and suddenly the spirit entered into me, and I was playing, but it was no longer me playing." [40]

> Porno For Pyros guitarist Peter DiStefano: "A lot of that guitar playing is not me. We figure we got help from something more powerful." [41]

> AC/DC guitarist Angus Young: "Someone else is steering me. I'm just along for the ride. I become possessed when I'm on stage." [42]

Rock singer and new television star, Ozzy Osbourne: "I don't know if I'm a medium for some outside force . . . Whatever it is, frankly, I hope it's not what I think — Satan." (43)

Famous composer Johann Sebastian Bach: "The end of all music should be the glory of God and the refreshment of the human spirit." (44)

That is how music started. It was created by God. It was created to glorify God, and in my opinion, I, as a Christian, should be only playing and listening to music that glorifies the Lord.

Now let's look at two more groups in a little more detail. The first group, or person, I want to look at is guitarist Jimi Hendrix. Hendrix is one of the most celebrated guitarists of all time. He had a tremendous influence on the world of rock 'n' roll. I have been in bands for a large part of my life and have spoken with numerous guitarists. When asked who inspired them, undoubtedly the name Jimi Hendrix came up. This includes Christian guitarists playing in Christian bands.

Hendrix appeared on *The Dick Cavett Show* on July 21, 1969, and had the following conversation with Cavett.

> Cavett: "Do you think music has a meaning?"
> Hendrix: "Oh yeah, definitely, it's getting to be more spiritual so then anything, uh, pretty soon I believe they are going to have to rely on music, to uh, like, get some sort of peace of mind, or satisfaction, direction actually." (45)

Hendrix, in a previous interview, stated: "The background of our music is a spiritual blues thing . . . We're making our music into 'electric church' music, a new kind of Bible you carry in your hearts (sic) . . . Rock is more than music; it's like church." (46) In describing the electric church to Cavett, Hendrix said, "That's just a belief that I have. We're playing for the sound to go inside the soul of the person actually, and see if we can awaken some kind of thing in their minds, you know, because there's so many sleeping people." [47]

Okay. There we have it. Music was very spiritual to Jimi Hendrix. He stated it was "a new Bible that you could carry in your heart." He said that his rock music was like "church," and that his music was played to "go inside the soul of people and awaken something in their mind."

So was Hendrix playing to Jesus? Was his music inspired by Jesus? You decide as you read these next few quotes.

Alan Douglas, the producer of a movie on the life of Hendrix, had this to say: "Now one of the biggest things about Jimi was . . . he believed that he was possessed by some spirit, and I got to believe it myself; and that's what we had to deal with all the time — he really believed it, and was wrestling with it constantly." [48] On that same note, girlfriend Faye Pridgon tells of Hendrix's battle with demons in more detail. She states, "He used to always talk about some devil or something was in him. You know, and he didn't have any control over it. He didn't know what made him act the way he acted and what made him say the things he said, **and songs and different things like that just came out of him** . . . (emphasis mine) He used to just grab his hair or something, or pull his hair or just stand in the mirror and cry . . . It seems to me he was so tormented and just torn apart and like he really was obsessed, you know, with something really evil . . . He said 'you're from Georgia . . . you should know how people drive demons out.' He used to talk about us going . . . and having some root lady or somebody see if she could drive this demon out of him." [49]

On September 17, 1970, Hendrix attended a dinner party in London. Later that night, he took nine sleeping pills mixed with the red wine he had already consumed. On September 18, he was pronounced dead. Cause of death was cited as "inhalation of vomit due to barbituate intoxication." [50] At the age of 25, Hendrix was another rock 'n' roll casualty.

The next group I want to talk about is the Rolling Stones. Yes, the Stones again. The Rolling Stones were on top of the rock world once the Beatles broke up. And in the late 1960s, one of their concerts would set a precedent for rock concerts of the future. Writer Donald Phau described the event as a "literal Satanic orgy," with "Mick Jagger, the leader of the Rolling Stones, playing the part of Lucifer." [51]

Over 400,000 people attended this particular concert, and by mid-morning a crowd had already begun to gather. The drug LSD was being passed around, and as author Tony Sanchez put it, "people were freaking out all over the place." He goes on to say, "Everybody was getting stoned out of his skull to pass the long hours before the music was to start — Mexican grass, cheap California wine, amphetamines . . ." [52] Sanchez continues with the following alarming information. A man high on acid tried to fly off a bridge. Another man sunk beneath the water in a drainage canal while "stoned" concertgoers merely looked on, watching as he drowned. According to Sanchez, doctors were also on the scene delivering babies to mothers who were "giving hysterical premature birth." [53]

The chaos continued. The Rolling Stones had hired the infamous motorcycle gang Hell's Angels to act as security for the concert. It was reported that "payment" was a mere $500 worth of free beer. Phau differs. He states, "Their real payment, however, was in drug sales. The Hell's Angels, an outlaw gang made up of robbers, rapists and murders, were the known controllers and sellers of drugs on the entire West Coast." [54]

What happened next is best described by Sanchez. When the Rolling Stones played, "strangely several of the kids were stripping off their clothes and crawling to the stage as if it were (sic) a high altar, there to offer themselves as victims for the boots . . . of the Angels. The more they were beaten and bloodied, the more they were impelled, as if by some supernatural force, to offer themselves as human sacrifices to these agents of Satan." [55]

In the front row of the crowd was a black man by the name of Meredith Hunter. Hunter would soon be singled out for a sacrifice. The Rolling Stones had just released their song "Sympathy for the Devil." The record had risen quickly up the charts to number one in the country. In the beginning of the song, lead singer Jagger introduces himself as Lucifer. The song was played, and the crowd began to dance wildly. [56]

What took place next is again best described by Sanchez, who states that a large member of the Hell's Angels walked over to Hunter and pulled his hair. A fight ensued and five more gang members came to help their friend. Hunter ran through the crowd. An "Angel" caught him and stabbed him in the back. Hunter then supposedly pulled out a gun and pointed it at the "Angel." Several members jumped Hunter and then stabbed him in the face and back repeatedly. When Hunter finally collapsed, several concertgoers tried to help him, but an "Angel" stood guard over him. "Don't touch him," he said menacingly. "He's going to die anyway, so just let him die." [57]

It was never proven that Hunter had a gun. Arrests were later made, but no one was indicted as no witnesses dared step forward against the "Angels." What did the Rolling Stones do? They continued to play "Sympathy for the Devil" as the entire group stood and watched Meredith Hunter being murdered. In addition, the murder was captured professionally by the crew filming the concert. The film, a box office hit, was released shortly after and can be rented at local video stores today. [58]

David Bowie did not realize how right he was when he said, "Rock has always been the devil's music . . . I believe that (it's) dangerous. It could well bring about a very evil feeling in the West . . . a dark era. I feel that we're only heralding something even darker than ourselves. [59] Even rock apologists acknowledge the dark side of rock 'n' roll. British magazine *MOJO* ran an article entitled "How Rock 'n' Roll Really Did Dance with the Devil." It stated, "The 1960s witnessed an 'occult revival,' the likes of which hadn't been seen in the West since . . . Aleister Crowley's Golden Dawn." [60]

Satan's purpose on earth is to stimulate lust within the human heart. Galatians 5:19-21 reads: "Now the works of the flesh are evident, which are: Adultery, fornication, uncleanness, lewdness, idolatry, sorcery, hatred, contentions, jealousies, out-bursts of wrath, selfish ambitions, dissensions, heresies, envy, murders, drunkenness, revelries, and the like; of which I tell you beforehand, just as I told you in time past, that those who practice such things will not inherit the kingdom of God." (61) In Bob Larson's book *Rock & Roll -- The Devil's Diversion,* he said, "Lyrics of today's songs are a large part of the cause of the tidal wave of promiscuity, venereal disease, illegitimate births and political upheaval that have recently swept over the country." He wrote that book in 1967. (62)

Today popular music is a $40 billion business. It sells everything from CDs and tapes to videos, stickers, posters, sweatshirts, underwear, and everything else imaginable. It is played everywhere. The fact is that there are 14.8 million teenagers in the U.S. today, and they buy the majority of popular music. (63) Research has shown that the average youth, from seventh to twelfth grade will listen to 11,000 hours of contemporary music, which is twice the time they will spend in the classroom. (64) Drug use among those 12 to 17 years old, has risen nearly 80 percent since 1992. In the last 15 years, teen suicide has risen 120 percent. Thirty-four percent of the teens have sex because the media makes it seem normal. Sin sells, and the world is buying. (65)

I could go into great detail about the recent school shootings and violence itself attached to popular music, but I won't because it has been written about by other authors. Eric Holmberg, maker of *Hells Bells* and *Hells Bells 2*, is a very gifted researcher. He found that one similarity in all these cases was an addiction to popular music. I simply want to bring up one particular case. (66)

Elyse Marie Pahler died at the age of 15. She was a virginal Christian who was sought out by three teenage boys. These boys gang raped, tortured, and used Elyse for a Satanic sacrifice, as they were attempting to commit the "ultimate sin against God" and buy their "ticket to hell." These young men had started their own rock band called Hatred, modeled after the popular band

Slayer, and they felt that this murder would help propel their band. Slayer has written songs such as "Spill the Blood," "Necrophiliac," and "Kill Again." Chris William, writer for the *Los Angeles Times*, said this of Slayer: "Nearly all (songs) deal with homicide, a fiery afterlife in hell, or a combination of the two . . . (They) aggressively mythologize mass murderers." (67)

This is just one tragic story from the present world. It is a glimpse at how music can affect the youth of today. This is not to say every kid will become a killer, but it also dispels the myth that it is harmless entertainment. Most youth will not take the music to that extreme. Yet how many teens will give into sexual temptation while listening to erotic lyrics? How many will experiment with drugs when they are made appealing by their favorite rock star? **These are the voices that are preaching to today's youth**. If the church is not aware and does not fight back, who will?

Music stars know the control they have over today's youth, and either do not care, or use it to their advantage. Shock rocker Marilyn Manson is quoted as saying, "If somebody kills themselves because of our music, then that's one less stupid person in the world." Noel Gallagher of the band Oasis is quoted as saying, "We're more popular than Jesus Christ now . . . I would hope we mean more to people than putting money in a church basket and saying 10 hail Marys on a Sunday." (68)

We set out in this chapter to determine whether music was powerful or not. I believe we can all overwhelmingly answer, "Yes, it is." Music can be used to provoke evil or to bless God. I admit there are some songs out there that are neutral. They talk of nonsense and have no apparent meaning. The song can be neutral, but what about the group? If a group promotes sex, drugs, alcohol and other idols that draw man away from God, the group is being used as a tool of the devil. I could write 1,000 pages about which group did what, but why do I need to? If you are truly a disciple of Christ, you are reading His word and you know it. You know it is not right to make light of adultery, or to glorify promiscuity, or to promote alcohol as an answer to one's problems.

Yet CHRISTIANS across this nation are listening to artists sing about it.

As we close this chapter, I would like you to consider my favorite psalm, Psalms 40:3, which reads, "He has put a new song in my mouth — praise to our God; Many will see it and fear, And will trust in the Lord." [69] A new song, not an old song, but a new one. See, God comes into our life and seeks to make a new creation. It is His wish that the old shall pass away. All of it. Even your music. He doesn't want anyone other then Him and His people to be your influence. And if you don't like that, you will have to argue with God

1. MatthewHenry, *Matthew Henry's Concise Commentary on the Whole Bible* (Nashville, Tennessee: Thomas Nelson, 1997), 278.
2. Steven Peters, *Truth About Rock* (Minneapolis: Bethany House, 1998), 13.
3. Michael Ventura, "Hear That Long Snake Moan," *Whole Earth Review* (Spring 1987) : 28, quoted in Eric Holmberg, *Hell's Bells 2: The Dangers of Rock 'n' Roll, 2001*, Reel 2 Real Ministries, video.
4. David Tame, *The Secret Power of Music*, 36, quoted in : *The Power Behind Anger Resolution: Dealing with Anger Addictions*, Session Nine, (Oak Brook, Illinois: Institute in Basic Life Principles, year), 10, www.iblp.org
5. Dr. Jack Wheaton, "Music that Murders," *Prophetic Observer* (2000), quoted in *The Power Behind Anger Resolution: Dealing with Anger Addictions*, Session Nine, (Oak Brook, Illinois: Institute in Basic Life Principles, year), 4, www.iblp.org
6. Dr. Jack Wheaton, "Music that Murders," *Prophetic Observer* (when in 2000?), quoted in *The Power Behind Anger Resolution: Dealing with Anger Addictions*, Session Nine, (Oak Brook, Illinois: Institute in Basic Life Principles, year), 11, www.iblp.org
7. Ibid.
8. Drs. Daniel and Bernadette Skubik, *The Neurophysiology of Rhythm*, quoted in *The Power Behind Anger Resolution: Dealing with Anger Addictions*, Session Nine, (Oak Brook, Illinois: Institute in Basic Life Principles, year), 1, www.iblp.org
9. Peters, *Truth About Rock*, 35.
10. Ibid.
11. Dr. Samuel Bacchiocchi, *The Christian and Rock Music: A Study of Biblical Principles of Music*, Chapter 5: "The Rock Rhythm and A Christian Response," quoted in *The Power Behind Anger Resolution: Dealing with Anger Addictions*, Session Nine, (Oak Brook, Illinois: Institute in Basic Life Principles, year), 10, www.iblp.org

12. *The Power Behind Anger Resolution: Dealing with Anger Addictions*, Session Nine, (Oak Brook, Illinois: Institute in Basic Life Principles, year), 11, www.iblp.org
13. Holmberg, *Hell's Bells 2*, video.
14. *The Closing of the American Mind*, Dr. Alan Bloom Bloom, 72, quoted in Holmberg, *Hell's Bells 2*, video.
15. Holmberg, *Hell's Bells 2*, video.
16. Ibid.
17. Ibid.
18. Bob Smithouser, *Chart Watch*, (Arcadia, California: Focus on the Family Publishers, 1998), 12.
19. http://www.members.tripod.com
20. Frank Thompson, *The Thompson Chain-Reference Bible: New International Version*, (Indianapolis, Indiana: B.B. Kirkbride Bbile Co., 1990)
21. Mickey Hart and Frederic Lieberman, *Spirit into Sound: The Magic of Music*, (Acid Test Productions,1999), 33, quoted in Holmberg, *Hell's Bells 2*, video.
22. Album liner notes from Michael Jackson's album *Dangerous*, quoted in Holmberg, *Hell's Bells 2*, video.
23. Steve Turner, *Hungry for Heaven*, (InterVarsity Press, 1995), 114, quoted in Holmberg, *Hell's Bells 2*, video.
24. Holmberg, *Hell's Bells 2*, video.
25. Hart and Lieberman, Spirit into Sound, 134, quoted in Holmberg, *Hell's Bells 2*, video.
26. Holmberg, *Hell's Bells 2*, video.
27. Ibid.
28. Stephen Davis, *Hammer of the Gods* (William Morrow & Co., Inc., 1985), 164, quoted in Holmberg, *Hell's Bells 2*, video.
29. Holmberg, *Hell's Bells 2*, video.
30. "Tori Amos," *Record Collector* Magazine (Nov.1999), quoted in Holmberg, *Hell's Bells 2*, video.
31. "Carlos Santana" Guitar Player magazine, (Nov. 1974), quoted in Holmberg, *Hell's Bells 2*, video.
32. *Rolling Stone* (March 16, 2000): 41, quoted in Holmberg, *Hell's Bells 2*, video.
33. Pastor Joe Schimmel, "Carlos Santana: Saint or Satanic?" http://www.goodfight.org/csantanaarticle.htm
34. *Rolling Stone* (March 16, 2000): 89, quoted in Holmberg, *Hell's Bells 2*, video.
35. Ibid.
36. *Rolling Stone* (March 16, 2000): 41, quoted in Holmberg, *Hell's Bells 2*, video.
37. *Rolling Stone* (March 16, 2000): 87, quoted in Holmberg, *Hell's Bells 2*, video.
38. Max Lucado, *The Inspirational Study Bible: New King James Version of the Bible*, (Dallas, Tx: Thomas Nelson, Inc., 1982.)
39. Ibid.

40. *Circus* (April, 1972): 38, quoted in Holmberg, *Hell's Bells 2*, video.
41. *Time* (July 5, 1998): 26, quoted in Holmberg, *Hell's Bells 2*, video.
42. Angus Young, (is this article title or author?) *Hit Parader* (??date??, 1985), quoted in Holmberg, *Hell's Bells 2*, video.
43. *Hit Parader* (February, 1976) quoted in Holmberg, *Hell's Bells 2*, video.
44. Holmberg, *Hells Bells*, video. (video #1??)
45. Holmberg, *Hell's Bells 2*, video.
46. Charles Murray, "Crosstown Traffic," (city, state: St. Martin's Press, 1989) 161 quoted in Holmberg, *Hell's Bells 2*, video.,
47. Holmberg, *Hell's Bells 2*, video.
48. http://www.sound/crock/hendrix1.1am
49. Ibid
50. Coral Amende, *Rock Confidential: A Backstage Pass to the Outrageous World of Rock 'n' Roll,* (New York, New York: Plume, 2000) 307.
51. Phau, "The Satanic Roots Of Rock," http://www.av1611.org/othpubls/roots.html, 13.
52. Sanchez, *Up and Down With the Rolling Stones*, 195.
53. Ibid.
54. Phau, "The Satanic Roots Of Rock," 13.
55. Sanchez, *Up and Down With the Rolling Stones*, 199.
56. Phau, "The Satanic Roots Of Rock," 13.
57. Sanchez, *Up and Down With the Rolling Stones*, 201, 202
58. Phau, "The Satanic Roots Of Rock," 14.
59. *Rolling Stone* (Feb. 12, 1976): 83, quoted in Holmberg, *Hell's Bells 2*, video.
60. *MOJO* (Sept.1999): 79, quoted in Holmberg, *Hell's Bells 2*, video.
61. *New King James Version of the Bible.*
62. Larson, Bob. *Rock & Roll: The Devil's Diversion* (McCook: Nebraska: 1967), 22.
63. Peters, Steven, *Truth About Rock* (Minneapolis: Bethany House, 1998) 20.
64. Holmberg, *Hells Bells 2*, video .
65. Stevens, *Truth About Rock*, 20.
66. Holmberg, *Hell's Bells 2*, video.
67. Smithouser, Bob, *Chart Watch*, Tyndale House Publishers, September 1998, 14.
68. Smithouser, Bob, *Chart Watch*, Tyndale House Publishers, September 1998 17.
69. *New King James Version of the Bible.*

Chapter 21

THE SIDEWALK

> "Mr. Recordman, do you know who I am?
> Mr. Recordman, do you really think I can?
> Sell a lotta records 'n' tour 'round the world,
> Make a lotta money 'n' meet lotsa girls
> Mr. Recordman, Mr. Recordman do you really think I can?
> It sounds like music to my ears
> I've dreamed of this for many years."
>
> "Mr. Recordman" by Ugly Kid Joe
> (http://www.purelyrics.com/index.php?lyrics=aoxqehzs)

The Sidewalk was also called the "meatmarket." I had transferred into this college town as a junior and all we had heard about was the "sidewalk." Cheap beer. Lots of girls. Dance music. Open seven nights. It was the bar across the street from our apartment. We thought we had it made!

I had moved to town to become a teacher. But in reality, I wanted to be a rock star. After realizing I would need to schmooze people, lie and be convincing, and play the role of the nice guy to make it the rock industry, I decided to study to become a politician. I was already well on my way to fitting that profile.

The Sidewalk was our playground. Evan and I would spend at least six nights a week there, if not seven. We watched *Monday Night Football* there. We went for laughs on Tuesday, which was gay night. Wednesday was the set up night for Thursday. Thursday was the "ultimate pick-up night." Friday was "towny night" — all the local (non-student) girls would come in. Saturday was also "towny" night. And Sunday was "oldies" night, when they played '50s rock. It was like clockwork.

I had a strategic plan all worked out. Evan and I would go to the Sidewalk and he would choose a girl that I had no chance of dating. My mission, if I chose to accept it, was to get her to go out with me. This required putting on a show that included a few of the following lines: "I am not the type to meet women in bars"; "So you and your boyfriend are in a long-distance relationship"; "You know I sing in a rock band"; "I am studying to be a lawyer"; "I was going to buy you a drink, but I don't want to insult you"; "I am going to be a politician"; "I am currently working on Senator so-and-so's campaign"; and a host of others. Most of all, I just listened to them as so very few other men did. I had become a "player."

Once I set up a date with one of these women, another system came into play. Evan and Andy kept a tally of the average amount of money I spent on a date. Through telling stories, making excuses, and flat out lying to these ladies, I kept the average down. When the year came to a close, the records showed 41 dates with 41 different women, with an average expenditure of 27 cents per date. I had perfected the scam.

None of these dates led to relationships. Absolutely none of then led to intimacy. It was merely "catch and release." It was a game. I had learned it while in high school, and as I mentioned before, it carried over into adult life. I found it rewarding to brag to the fellows, but yet I felt empty inside. I had failed to realize that I was playing with people's emotions and toying with their relationships. The majority of them had boyfriends, but I didn't care. To me I was only having fun. I was sowing my wild oats, I was just being a boy, I was going through a stage, and all the other clichés the world offers to explain my behavior.

Those girls (at least most of them) knew I was a "player" or "scammer," but they didn't care. I would be out with one, and have another walk up and say, "Don't date him. He is a scammer." I would sheepishly laugh and then quickly make up a story. I wanted to be a rock star. I was becoming like my idols. I was becoming like the men I looked up to on MTV. All I needed was some musicians that could stay out of rehab and jail. All I needed was a record contract. "Mr. Recordman, Mr. Recordman, do you know who I am?"

"For we ourselves were also once foolish, disobedient, deceived, serving various lusts and pleasures, living in malice and envy, hateful and hating one another."

Titus 3:3

Chapter 22

COVERED UP

> "Tonight I wanna give it all to you
> In the darkness
> There's so much I wanna do
> And tonight I wanna lay it at your feet
> 'Cause girl, I was made for you
> And girl, you were made for me
> I was made for loving you baby
> You were made for lovin' me."
>
> "I Was Made for Lovin' You" by Kiss
> (http://www.lyricsfreak.com/k/kiss/16725.htm)

Roses. Hershey's Kisses. Make-up. Girls. All of them would be combined that night. We were headed back to the finals of the battle of the bands. We had won the preliminaries dressed up as the rock band Kiss, mouthing the song "I Was Made for Lovin' You Baby."

As we entered the bar, the bouncer laughed. Our faces were totally covered in make-up, and we were all decked out in boots, spandex suits and glitter. He had no idea who was under that make-up, so it was useless to card us. He just smiled and let us in.

Before we could even set up our stuff, we were mobbed. People shook our hands and followed us like we were gods. Girls swarmed us. It was very flattering, yet borderline disgusting. Some of these young women were asking us to take them home for the evening, and it wasn't for prayer. They were very forward in describing where they wanted to go, and what they wanted to do. It confused me. I realized they were fascinated by this whole rock and roll thing, but these women had just about as much idea of who we were as the bouncer did. It came to a point where we had to restrain them.

Finally our name was called, and we went up to play. The crowd went crazy. I, playing the part of Gene Simmons, was shooting fire out of my mouth and drooling fake blood down the front of me. You would think this would be revolting to a woman who was in search of a man, but not that night. People lose their minds at these concerts. The aforementioned changes begin to take place in their bodies, and their "flight or fight" response kicks in. The music drives them to lose their inhibitions and they begin to "flesh out their destinies," in the words of Aleister Crowley.

Let's not miss the point here. These women did not give two hoots about me. They wanted Gene Simmons. In fact, the majority of them called me "Gene." They had watched him on TV or attended his concerts and were drawn in by his presence. This is a man who claims to have slept with 2,000 women in a 10-year period. This is a man who brags about having illegitimate children. He proudly plays songs about degrading women. Yet these women adore him. Anyone who says that this music has no effect on people needs to check back into reality. Simmons once stated that the people at his concerts would do anything he told them to do. I felt that same power when I played the part of Simmons. It was unbelievable.

This was a mock rock concert in a bar in a small college town in mid-Michigan, yet the "fans" were still reacting. It is only magnified in the real rock and roll world, where bands perform in stadiums in front of thousands. At the time, their actions astounded me. Now it all made sense.

We finished the night by throwing out Hershey's Kisses to the crowd and passing out roses. We then sat and quietly waited for the votes to be tallied. We danced wildly when they announced we had won, and quickly went to retrieve our trophy. We received our award of $50 and immediately turned it over to the bar for alcohol, another bondage of this lifestyle.

The five of us in the band stumbled out unharmed that night. Or at least we thought we did. We managed to elude those women in hot pursuit and escape to the safety of our apartments. Part of me enjoyed the power that night and yet part of me was scared. I had experienced satan's power previously and had felt the same mixed emotions. I wanted to be powerful, but the Lord was chasing me and would give me glimpses of where this power was going to take me.

I was headed toward judgment day, and the make-up wasn't going to help. The Lord sees beyond the make-up, beyond the power, and beyond the music. There I would be, on bended knee, confessing to Jesus as Lord before I entered hell. Thank God it happened on this side of the grave.

"That at the name of Jesus every knee should bow, of those in heaven, and of those on earth, and of those under the earth, and that every tongue should confess that Jesus Christ is Lord, to the glory of God the Father."
                                                   Philippians 2:10, 11

Chapter 23

THE VOW. . .

> ". . . and the road becomes my bride
> I have stripped of all but pride
> so in her I do confide
> and she keeps me satisfied
> gives me all I need . . .
> but I'll take my time anywhere
> free to speak my mind anywhere
> and I'll redefine anywhere . . .
> Anywhere I may roam . . ."
>
> "Wherever I May Roam" by Metallica
> (http://www.elyrics.net)

"What are you doing Saturday?" Eddie asked inquisitively. "Probably working," I answered. "Why?" We both knew I had the night off, but no way was I going to spend it with him. Eddie had always been a punk to me. He had the idea that he would someday run the Boomerang nightclub. He had been head of security there for some time when I hired on. But he had one problem — the boss thought he was lazy. The truth has a way of catching up with you.

I had been working at the Boomerang for three months when the boss asked to see me. "I want you to be the head of security," he said. I nodded approvingly and we shook hands. I had found favor in his eyes. Three months earlier he had told me I was too small to be a bouncer in a town full of football players. I assured him it took more then strength to run his bar. It had proven to be true.

Of course this didn't sit well with Eddie, and he became even lazier, if that was possible. He was downright rude at times, and I eventually chose to have nothing to do with him. That is why I wondered why he wanted to hang out with me on a Saturday night. "I have the deal of a lifetime for you," Eddie stated. I raised my eyebrows as an indication to continue. "I can set you up to be a roadie for Metallica." My heart beat faster. Was this for real? "Are you serious?" I stammered. "Yeah, I have seven roadie spots for the local concert in Saginaw."

I stood amazed. Eddie's friend was supposed to do it, but suddenly backed out. This, to me, was a chance of a lifetime. We were going backstage. We were going to meet the band! "Count me in for sure!" I said. I could put up with Eddie for one night to get closer to my dream.

There was some confusion regarding set-up time, so the stage was already constructed when we arrived. They told us we would tear it down instead. In the meantime, we had open passes to the concert and were allowed to go anywhere we wanted. We watched the concert in awe, merely a few feet from the stage. It was the typical scene — booze, drugs and women. Legend had it that in the rock and roll world, bands would have lots of ladies backstage after the concert. I would soon realize it was not a tale.

The concert ended and we were ushered backstage. "Where's the band?" we asked. "They'll be out in a while," we were told, but first we had to tear down the stage. For the next four hours we were herded like cattle as we filled semi after semi with their gear. I was working the backstage area and quite frankly looking for a break when I heard Eddie yell, "Mike get over here! You're are not gonna believe this."

Eddie led me through the building to the front stage. I turned the corner to see a group of laughing guys huddled together. They were looking at photos set up like a wall of fame, with the words "For the Boys" above them. I walked closer. To my amazement, I saw an endless display of Polaroids of naked women. They most likely had been taken backstage, and the collection had grown over time. I guess it was a parting gift from the band.

Moments later, the band walked past us without even giving a nod. They were busy trying to avoid a group of 15 autograph seekers who had stood in the rain for four hours. They had snubbed us, but I didn't care. We had witnessed the scene. It was true, it was really true — money, booze, women. It was rock and roll and life on the road. I was going to enjoy it "wherever I may roam."

**"There is a way that seems right to a man,
But its end is the way of death."   Proverbs 14:12**

Chapter 24

STONED

> "I'm havin' a ball hatin' every little thing about you! . . .
> I get sick when I'm around
> I can't stand to be around
> I hate everything about . . . you!"
>
> "Everything About You" by Ugly Kid Joe
> (www.lyricsfreak.com)

It was 4:30 a.m., but the light was still on at Heidi's. Joe had been trying to call his girlfriend for over an hour, but she didn't answer. There had been a small riot across town and he wanted to make sure she was okay. He picked up pebbles and began to toss them at her window. At 4:30 a.m., the last thing he expected to see in her upstairs bedroom window was my face. I was a dead man.

Returning from a date at 3:30 a.m., I went to see Heidi. She and I had been "friends" behind her boyfriend's back for about six months. When she told me she had to stop seeing me, I pretended to hate her. It was my first date with someone else and I wanted to rub it in her face. Heidi's brother was in town and she figured he was the one throwing the rocks. "Open the window and tell him I'll be right down," she told me. We both shook in fear when I said, "It's Joe."

We stood in the hallway of the second floor and try to concoct a story. She told me to hide in one of her roommate's rooms until the coast was clear. I reminded her there was one way in and one way out of her house, and her huge boyfriend was going to hunt until he found me. Joe was still locked outside, now throwing large handfuls of rocks against the house.

I know it was only maybe 30 seconds or so in total, but time seemed to stand still in that hallway. Several thoughts flashed through my mind. I hadn't even held Heidi's hand that night. "Joe is wrong to be angry," I reasoned, as we were just talking. I could tell him that, but it appeared Joe was not ready to talk. I could run,

- 97 -

but there was nowhere to go. I thought I could fight, but Joe was big and mad. Then I thought, "I deserve to be punished. I've been dating this guy's girlfriend for six months." Those insights were all right-on . . . all but one. Joe did have a right to be angry. I wanted to run from my sin and say "not guilty." I needed to fight, but not with Joe. I did deserve punishment. In the end, my only thoughts were, "I'm a dead man," and, "I want my Dad."

Heidi finally unlocked the door and gave Joe a push that would have made most pro football players jealous. I ran, I tripped, and I crawled the entire way home. Then I hid behind the door like a coward, picked up the phone, and called my Dad. I deserved to be punished that night, but I was spared. Yet I spent the next three months hiding from Joe.

I was a long way from God that night, but His principles were all around me. My sin had caught up with me, I was headed for death, and I had no Father to save me. I was only a heartbeat away from His judgment. Nowadays life is different. I don't hide when the enemy comes knocking; instead I stand and fight. But first I drop and call on my Father in heaven. While I still deserve punishment for less serious offenses, because of Him, I am spared death again.

". . . be sure your sin will find you out."
Numbers 32:23

Chapter 25

IN CHAINS

> "In the beginning God made the land
> Then He made the water and creatures, then he made man
> He was born with a passion, love and hate
> A restless spirit with a need for a mate
> But there was somethin' missin', somethin' lost
> So he came with the answer, here's what it cost
> One part love, one part wild
> One part lady, one part child
> I give you women! women!
> Lots of pretty women (men, men)
> They can't live without them . . .
> Skin on skin,
> Let the love begin . . .
> Hair, eyes, skin on skin . . .
> (legs) legs
> (thighs) thighs
> What's that spell? . . .
> (women) oh we can't live without them."
>
> "Women" by Def Leppard
> (www.lyricsfreak.com)

Women consumed me. It was the thrill of victory. The thrill of achieving the much sought after goal of seeing what my eyes had undressed so many times before. I woke up thinking of women, and went to bed thinking of women. Every waking moment of every day, my mind was consumed with women.

When I woke up in the morning, I would make my plan. I would simply survive until I could call her, or stall until I could go see her. If there was not a "her," I lived for other things. I would live to go to the bar and pick up a girl, or to go to a party and ask one out. I would not include myself in any social event unless it involved women. It didn't matter to me if she had a boyfriend, fiancé, or even a husband, as long as there was someone to flirt with.

In high school and I had received good grades. I had graduated from one college and two universities with excellent grades. Yet the only knowledge I pursued was that of women. Beyond wanting to be a baseball player, beyond wanting to be a rock and roll star, and beyond wanting to be famous, I wanted women. The music had led me down a slippery slope of no return. It made me think of women, it helped me get women, and it encouraged me to lust after women. I was brainwashed. When I visited my family and brought a girl home with me, no one ever said, "See you later," because they knew she wasn't coming back. My game had become one of "catch and release," and it lasted for 14 years.

Our Father in heaven admitted in Genesis 2:18 that it is normal for a man to have desire for a woman. That verse reads, "And the Lord God said, it is not good that the man should be alone; I will make him an help meet for him." The devil seeks to pervert whatever God has ordained for man. This includes the exchange of "lust" for "love."

Each man seeks to worship something, and I, through the influence of music, had chosen women. Not until I had surrendered my entire life to Jesus Christ did I began to realize that women were more than a "trophy" to show off to my friends. Father God gave me a new heart the day I believed in Him and slowed my racing state of mind to a pace I could tolerate without having a nervous breakdown. The bondage of lust had been growing in me for 15 years when I met Jesus. I had developed many carnal ideas about women, and every time Father God revealed another one to me, I immediately took on a great deal of shame. The shame was not God's intent, but rather He willed that I would become free from carnal thinking. We worked on them one at a time and eventually the scales tipped to righteousness.

Then God showed me Kelli. Through prayer and surrender to Christ, my Father in heaven has supplied what I once thought unachievable. He has given me a woman to "love." God has brought into my life a wonderful human being. She is the kind of woman that makes every guy around me wonder how I ever talked her into marrying me. She is a woman of high standards and morals. She is a woman who stands up for what is right, and protects those who cannot fight for themselves. She is simply the most beautiful (inside and out), most understanding, and most elegant woman I have ever met. She is a lady, and I have done absolutely nothing to deserve her. Thank you, Father, for changing me.

"Charm is deceitful and beauty is passing, But a woman who fears the Lord, she shall be praised."
Proverbs 31:30

Chapter 26

THE JUNGLE

> "Welcome to the jungle
> We take it day by day
> If you want it you're gonna bleed
> But it's the price you pay
> And you're a very sexy girl
> That's very hard to please
> You can taste the bright lights
> But you won't get them for free
> In the jungle, welcome to the jungle
>
> "Welcome to the Jungle" by Guns N' Roses
> (http://www.mygnr.com/lyrics/2-1.html)

Long hair, dangling earring, a fifth of vodka, a pint of peach schnapps, and two tickets to the Metallica and Guns N' Roses concert. What more could two guys ask for? At least that is what we thought at the time.

Daimon had received two tickets for the concert as a birthday present from his girl. Luckily for me, he dumped her right before the concert. We loaded the car and headed for the show. It was a four-and-a-half hour drive and we planned on unloading the contents of the bottles on the way there.

We arrived a few minutes early and staggered across the I-75 freeway into the Pontiac Silverdome. We sat on the end opposite the stage. Rock band Faith No More was playing, and as with most any other warm-up band, no one was listening. I had been to see Ozzy. I had been to see Metallica. I had been to see more bands then I could count. But never before had I been to a multifeatured band event. These events were said to be a little more wild and crazy. I figured it was due to the long day and all the excess party time. Because of the massive stages the bands called for, it would take the roadies (the band's crew) more than an hour to set up the next back drop. With all that downtime, something was bound to happen.

Metallica played their full ear-blasting set. We danced. We yelled. We screamed. And of course, we lusted over women. We then kicked back in our seats in anticipation of a wild Guns N' Roses concert. What we didn't know is that they were not going to be the true "main" attraction.

The lights came on and the roadies went to work. But something was peculiar. In the center of the arena floor was a man on a 50-foot skylift. He sat there perched like a buzzard searching for prey. He had a news camera, and soon the object he was filming was shown on the big screen.

The cameraman panned from one beautiful woman to the next. Every half-drunk male in the arena became suddenly sober. Suddenly, the camera stopped. The woman on the big screen smiled and waved, and then, much to the delight of the 25,000 plus males, she removed her shirt. Then another woman did. Then another, and another. Each women he showed on camera complied. Before long, 14- and 15-year-old girls were joining in. I turned to Daimon and said, "This is only going to get worse."

As more women removed their tops, you could see hands on the screen coming from everywhere. Men were accosting women, and some of it not to their delight. Next, women began to remove their pants and undergarments. This also continued from woman to woman. And then, for the sake of decency, I will just say it got worse than a pornographic movie. ALL ON THE BIG SCREEN. It was beyond reality. Men began to lose their minds. Women were being held up in the air while the men below them fondled them. I was suddenly glad we had horrible seats and were so far removed from the action. The scene got uglier . . . and then the lights went out.

We heard the screeching voice of Guns N' Roses frontman Axle Rose scream, "Oh, I love Detroit." This was far from funny. This went way beyond lust. It was scary. Fights broke out, tempers flared, and the whole crowd was in a frenzy. Guns N` Roses' music began horribly. Most likely they had partied all day too. I said to Daimon, "Let's go," as we sprinted for the car. Inside and outside the crowd was chanting, "GNR sucks," and a riot was beginning in the parking lot. I was honestly glad to make it out alive.

I was nowhere near God that night, but something in me was starting to change. I had always wanted to be the one on the stage, the one in the limelight. But that night I wouldn't have given a plug nickel to be part of it. To look back now, given the lyrics of the bands, the mental state of the crowd, the massive amount of alcohol and drugs being consumed, the "halftime show," and the people these events attracted, it all added up to a nightmare. The year was 1990. Today, not only are concerts like this the norm, but they are actually more violent.

While describing the type of crowds his band draws, Motley Crue star Nikki Six stated, "Quite a few times girls have been raped at our concerts. Some have claimed to have gone deaf while we were onstage. Someone lost their eyes in a fight. So we get assault charges because we were onstage when they got the sh-t kicked out of them. It goes on and on." [1]

In 2001, Crowd Management Strategies did a study of 31 concerts and found the following: 55 deaths, 11,438 injuries and 418 arrests. [2] One of the biggest causes of the problems are "mosh pits." Mosh pits are a hole in the floor that some concertgoers climb into and then slam into the walls and into each other. Concertgoer Josh Simon states, "A lot of times people lose teeth and are trampled in the pit. The first show I ever went to I got kicked in the face." [3]

I have already talked about the violence at the Rolling Stones concert in chapter 20, but 10 years later 11 people were killed at a Who concert. They were rushing forward to get the best seats. In 1996, a girl was crushed to death at a Smashing Pumpkins concert. In 2000, nine fans were killed rushing to the stage at a Pearl Jam concert. In 2001, a surging crowd at a Limp Bizkit concert left one girl dead of an apparent heart attack. [4] Yet *Billboard* magazine senior editor Ray Waddell still states, "In terms of activities one can engage in, rock concerts are one of the safest things you can do." [5] If you go by the statistics, each concert results in 1.77 deaths, 368.96 injuries and 13.48 arrests. [6] Safe? In comparison to what? Sorry, I don't buy it.

> **"Can a man take fire to his bosom, and his clothes not be burned?"**
>
> **Proverbs 6:27**

1. Coral Amende, *Rock Confidential* (city, state: Plume Books, 2000), 265.
2. Kelly Kolyer, "Concertgoers Risk Injury in Pit, Stands," *The Black & White Online: In-Depth*, http://www.waltwhitman.edu/blackandwhite/archives/413/depth4.html,1.
3. Ibid.
4. Steve Gorman, "Great White Fire Ranks as Rock's worst Tragedy," http://news.yahoo.com/news?tmpl=story2&cid=638&ncid=762=2&u=/nm/20030222/en, 2.
5. Steve Gorman, "Great White Fire Ranks as Rock's worst Tragedy, http://news.yahoo.com/news?tmpl=story2&cid=638&ncid=762=2&u=/nm/20030222/en, 3.
6. Kelly Kolyer, "Concertgoers Risk Injury in Pit, Stands," *The Black & White Online: In-Depth*, http://www.waltwhitman.edu/blackandwhite/archives/413/depth4.html,1.

Chapter 27

HERO

"When you see the day gettin' darker
You can run to your lies, run to your cover
When you feel the heat from a lover
You hit the highway lookin' for another."

"Nothin' For Nothin'" by Cinderella
(www.lyricsfreak.com)

I met her at work. She was the big catch in the pond. Everyone had their line cast and I was not to be outdone. She looked just like Alyssa Milano from the television show *Who's the Boss?* and had determination like Potiphar's wife. I ran the wrong way.

Lera grew up in a broken home, with a mother who had her own life and a father whose only concern was pictures of dead presidents. She had been around the block and back twice, but I didn't care. It was all about image, presenting a trophy, and beating the other guy to the punch. I pursued women like a prized hockey player pursues the Stanley Cup.

I calculated expenditures, risks, time commitments, public appearances and, regrettably, fringe benefits. Lera would not be an exception. The world passed by, work days ran one into another, time with friends became minimal, and family time was an afterthought in the all consuming quest for the ultimate in bachelorhood: to be seen with the "most stunning physical specimen" in the area.

Our relationship was pathetic at best. She would far too often hang out with "friends" and "accidentally" become promiscuous with them. I forgave her time and time again. As long as she kept quiet, my reputation would remain untarnished and my appearances with her would be profitable. It did not matter to me that she was unfaithful as I would repay her with the same, in another town, where once again I would work the "system." No matter where I was, there had to be an exceptionally beautiful girl there with me. If not, what was the point?

With Lera, there was need for damage control and coverups. I had even instituted a system for answering questions about past relationships. I would either tell my newfound love that the previous girl was a "psycho" who was infatuated with me, or I would simply deny dating the women. In this case, I chose the latter, and was busted with little chance of redeeming myself. Lera's mother had seen me out with the very girl that I denied ever dating. My only choice was to say that her mother was lying.

Then came the meeting. I sat with Lera at my side and stared into the face of my accuser. Lera's mother proceeded to tell the story of how she had seen me with this other girl and that she could prove it was true. I smiled in the manner I had learned from studying my favorite politicians. I said, "I'm sorry ma'am, but you are wrong." She pressed on until I cleared my throat and said to Lera, "She's lying, your mom is lying."

I had dated the girl one night and had a horrible time. I was embarrassed to admit it and chose the lie to be more rewarding. Lera didn't believe me, but I didn't care. I had kept my reputation intact. I wouldn't dare admit the fact that I had made the mistake of having a less than successful date. That would infer weakness, something that a man whose entire life is a game cannot afford to expose.

As I now look back on that day, I realize I was merely a pawn in a much bigger game. The devil had big plans for me. He had invested a lot of time and was betting that his investment would pay off. I'm sure it did to some extent, but his victory was cut short on Calvary's hill. Joseph ran from Potiphar's wife, I ran to her. Both of us ended up in prison. His was literal, mine was spiritual. God showed him a way out, and He showed me a way out. I wanted to be a hero in man's eyes, Joseph wanted to be one in God's. Joseph became one in both.

"And the patriarchs, becoming envious, sold Joseph into Egypt (slavery). But God was with him "and delivered him out of all his troubles, and gave him favor and wisdom . . ."

Acts 7:9-10a

Chapter 28

BOOMERANG

"I wrote her off for the tenth time today
And practiced all the things I would say
But she came over
I lost my nerve
I took her back and made her dessert
Now I know I'm being used . . .
That's okay cause I've got no self esteem . . .
When she's saying that she wants only me
Then I wonder why she sleeps with my friends . . .
Late at night she knocks on my door
Drunk again and looking to score
Now I know I should say no
But that's kind of hard when she's ready to go
I may be dumb but I'm not a dweeb
I'm just a sucker with no self esteem."

"Self Esteem" by Offspring
(http://www.musicsonglyrics.com)

    I tried them out when I was a little tike and they never worked. They were usually those 50- cent plastic boomerangs from the local Ben Franklin store. Maybe I didn't throw them right. Maybe I just got what I paid for. I didn't understand the concept, but years later I began to get it.

    I had sown a lot of bad seed. As I stated before, I had dated women who had boyfriends. I dated women who had fiancées. I had even tried to date women who were married. I ignored my own girlfriends. I failed to call them when I promised. I was dishonest with them. And I was unfaithful. But then, something happened.

    I met Sharon, I met Kelsey, I met Theresa, I met Heidi and I met Corrine. Although I met each of them at different times, the result was the same. These were women I thought I loved. Obviously, without God in my life, I failed to realize what "true love" was. These women lied. These women ignored me. They "forgot" to call. They were unfaithful. The boomerang had come back and hit me in the face, and I did not like it. It was a lesson I needed to learn.

The pain was overwhelming. Each time it happened, I had all the clues right in front of my face. Yet when I found out that they had cheated, it stunned me. I wept. I stopped eating. I became enraged to the point of fits. And then I wept again. Back then I would say, "She has broken my spirit." I would make up all these things in my mind that I was going to tell them, then I'd freeze up when I saw them. They would act like nothing happened, and eventually I would take them back. I had lost my self-esteem.

I would put up with their lies. I would put up with their mental torture. I would put up with them ignoring me. I would put up with their cheating. The tables had now turned. I was reaping what I had sown. And while I didn't like it, I figured I deserved it. I was truly getting what I had paid for.

"Do not be deceived, God is not mocked; for whatever a man sows, that he will also reap."
Galatians 6:7

Chapter 29

THE CIGAR

> "I got bruises on my memory
> I got tear stains on my hands
> And in the mirror there's a vision
> Of what used to be a man
> I'm a thousand miles from nowhere
> Time don't matter to me
> 'Cause I'm a thousand miles from nowhere
> And there's no place I want to be."
>
> "A Thousand Miles from Nowhere" by Dwight Yoakam
> (http://www.sing365.com)

The door was cracked open and I was slumped in my seat. I can remember the soft wind blowing against my face that morning. I had just arrived home from working the night shift. My roommates were inside sleeping, unaware that I was even home. I stayed outside in my brand new truck and felt unloved.

As I sat there and sucked on my Swisher Sweet Cigar, I mulled over the last year of mistakes. My poor choices had left me lonely, broke and numb. It seemed that I had borrowed money from every hand I shook, cried on every available shoulder offered, and replayed every hopeless episode over and over in my head.

I had drunk every drink, slow danced with every love, pushed every button, rolled every die, and bet every chip. I was tired. Of course I had worked the night shift, but my fatigue went far beyond that. I was tired of running, too tired to care, too tired to fight and too tired to cry. In my eyes, I was unloved. Another puff. I felt empty.

I had always hated cigars, but I often did things to make me feel tougher. You do that when you have low self-esteem. You become someone else, you keep running. But not today. This would be the end. Enough is enough. Another puff. How could I have done that? How could she have done that? Why does it have to hurt so bad? Why doesn't she forgive me? Why did she lie? Why didn't I just shut up? Why couldn't she show she cared? Why didn't she call? Why didn't I listen? Another puff. I'll just borrow Travis's gun. He will never suspect a thing. Heck, I'll even buy it if he'll sell it. That way there is no guilt. One quick motion. One quick end. Another puff. I can do this. I have the courage. No good-bye, no drama, no show. Just one simple pull of the trigger and it's over. My problems will be over, and I'll be free. Free forever. The last puff.

I ground out the butt and felt relieved. I had finally made a decision. Today was the day. But then the door opened. Geoffrey walked outside and lit up his smoke. He finished his morning stretch and rubbed his sleepy eyes. "What are you doing out here?" he asked. "Just thinking," I answered. "Get in the house and get some rest," he replied. I nodded and did so.

Geoffrey still doesn't know it, but he helped save my life that day. In the middle of making up my mind, he interrupted me. He walked through that door and interrupted me. My life had been saved for another day.

A short time later, I sat in a different seat. They were standing, I was sitting. They were singing, I was sitting. Then the door opened. The song went, "Shout to the Lord, all the earth let us sing. Power and majesty praise to the King. Mountains bow down and the seas will roar at the sound of Your name." It finally broke. I wasn't tired anymore. Tears began to run down my cheek. I was crying. As they sang, "Nothing compares to the promise I have in You," I tugged on her shirt. I said, "I'm ready, Momma," to my godmother, and she took me by the hand to the altar. He was knocking, and before I knew it, I had reached out my hand and opened the door. Jesus walked in. He said, "Come in My house and rest." My life had been saved for eternity.

Like I said, I hated cigars. They stunk. They tasted horrible. And as they get older, they fall apart. Twenty-nine years I had been burning. The stench of my sin had been horrible in the nostrils of my Father in heaven. My fruit was horrible to the taste. And my life was totally unraveled. Yet he still loved me. He stepped in that morning and put out the fire. He breathed life into my lungs. I was truly free. And that is why I love Him.

"For God so loved the world that He gave His only begotten Son, that whoever believes in Him should not perish but have everlasting life."

John 3:16

Chapter 30

THE LAST SONG

> "There is no escape
> And that is for sure
> This is the end we won't take any more
> Say goodbye
> To the world you live in
> You have always been taking
> But now you're giving
> Running,
> On our way
> Hiding,
> You will pay
> Dying,
> One thousand deaths
> Searching,
> Seek and destroy."
>
> "Seek and Destroy" by Metallica
> (www.lyricsfreak.com)

    Practice was about half finished and I was feeling the power. The black light was barely visible through the smoke-filled garage. The next song on the list was "Seek and Destroy" by Metallica. It was my favorite to sing. The throaty vocals gave the impression that the singer had smoked since the age of six. The room was filled with girls, most of whom were tag-alongs with Chad (the guitarist) and Juan (the drummer). They would make up the audience other than a junior high-looking male. I figured he was someone's kid brother, and he was.
    I had given my life to Jesus about four months ago and a break-up of the band was inevitable. Somehow it didn't seem right to cuss anymore and the same ol' conversations were beginning to feel out of place. God had been moving in on my life.
    I (through the power of Jesus) had been able to overcome many obstacles in the months prior, but the draw to music was still strong. The boys picked up their axes (guitars) and began to wail through the two-minute intro. My whole body trembled from the beat of the drum and the euphoric rush of being the center of attention. The singer is always the frontman. With that position

comes pressure, control and the power of the band. At every concert I had ever attended I looked at the stage and thought, "that is going to be me." I would have honestly sold my soul to be famous. AC/DC (Anti-Christ/Devil Child) sang about the difficulty of reaching fame in their song "It's a Long Way to the Top if You Want to Rock and Roll." I was willing to go the extra mile.

My part began and I belted out the lyrics with pride. It is a long song that escalates into a fury of screeching guitars, smashing drums, crashing cymbals and screaming words. Then in an instant, it stops. It was always the last song we played before our break, and today would be no different. I set down the microphone, said thank you to compliments, and headed out for some fresh air.

On my way out, I nodded to the kid, all the while thinking, "Someday this kid can be like me." I never realized my thoughts would play out in reverse. The kid stopped me to say something, and I graciously turned to thank him, anticipating a compliment. "Do you like this music?" he asked. With a raised eyebrow I answered, "Well, yeah," with a condescending tone. "I used to," he continued, "but then I stopped." I nodded with approval as a gesture to continue. "I stopped listening because the Lord Jesus Christ delivered me from it," he said. I froze.

For seconds I stood there and stared at the floor as tears welled up in my eyes. I walked over to Chad and said, "I quit, man." I grabbed my coat and walked out. I drove away that night knowing I had made the right choice. I was crying, but the tears of sorrow soon turned to tears of joy. I have never seen that kid since that day, but I was right about what I assumed. He was somebody's kid brother. He was Jesus'.

"For it is the God who commanded light to shine out of darkness, who has shone in our hearts, to give the light of the knowledge of the glory of God in the face of Jesus Christ."

2 Corinthians 4:6

Chapter 31

THE NEW SONG

*"Many times, I've failed you in the past,
I went off and did my own thing,
But every time you forgave me of my sin
and that's why I can't help but sing."*

"Your Love is Unconditional" by Christ For The Nations Institute
(Patrick Knock & Eduardo Coronado)

For those first few moments I felt out of place. It certainly was not where I had figured I would end up. I shared my testimony with my church family previously, but as famous Christian author and pastor T.D. Jakes says, there is a part of your testimony you haven't shared with anyone. I figured if they knew everything, they would not have even let me up on the stage. I had been a drunk. I had been a womanizer. I had been an adulterer. I had been a liar. I began to think there was no reason that I should have been up on stage, but then I felt the peace of God come over me. I realized that He had forgiven me of my sins, and suddenly I wanted to sing.

It had been five years since I was saved, and I had always made it a point to not get involved with singing. I had spent so much time developing my singing talent with the devil, that I did not wish to open any other door that he might slip through. But, my beautiful, encouraging wife had other ideas. Kelli had heard me sing without embarrassment at home. She'd say, "You need to sing for the Lord outside these walls." I would laugh at her, and tell her to be quiet. Yet deep down inside I was afraid. I had always wanted to be the frontman in the world, the center of attention, and wow people with my voice. Thank God it never seemed to work out. Every time we got a band together, something would happen to break it up.

I kept singing at home and Kelli kept pushing. One night she returned from praise and worship practice with some news. Kelli, who has a beautiful voice, had told the worship leader that I wanted to sing a special song. I panicked. For a week I sweated it out and tried to decide how I could get out of it. There was no way I could stand up in front of all those people and sing, especially sober.

Three days before I was to audition, I called the worship leader and asked for a private audition. Don't think that messing up the song on purpose didn't cross my mind. I figured if I could convince the worship leader that I was a horrible singer, she would ask me not to sing. The time came and I sang for her in my normal voice, but with very little volume. She must have thought it was at least presentable for the church congregation.

During rehearsal, I had to sing in front of the entire praise team. I am known throughout the area for being a smart-aleck, and I figured they were going to use this opportunity for my redemption. No one laughed, no one teased, and no one grimaced in agony. That meant the song was a keeper.

Sunday morning arrived. The team finished all the praise and worship songs without me, and I thought I was home free. But then came time to take up the offering. My pastor had joked relentlessly over the years that I was going to sing, much to everyone's enjoyment. So when he announced on that Sunday that I was going to sing, everyone again laughed. I stood up and walked to the stage. I could feel every muscle in my body tighten as I picked up the microphone. At that moment, I would have rather been anywhere else than in that church. My good friend from Bible school, Mark Stahl, was in town to hold a revival and was taking part in our service. I was petrified to sing in front of Mark, my parents, and all my Christian brothers and sisters. But I realized that my best friend died on a cross so I could be free, and I figured the least I could do was sing for Him. I whispered, "Lord this is for you. Please anoint my voice so that it will draw your people into worship. And Lord, please keep me from throwing up."

Seconds later, the music started and I began to sing. The church erupted with praise for the Lord. People were whooping and hollering and dancing and singing. God had answered my prayer. When the song came to an end, the house erupted again, this time with applause. I hugged a few people, thanked several others for their compliments, and then made my way out of the sanctuary. As I then walked out those sanctuary doors and down to the church kitchen, I said, "Thank you, Lord, for allowing me to sing," and I heard a still, small voice reply, "Well done." Once in the kitchen, I got on my knees and wept like a baby. In chapter 30, entitled "The Last Song," I was full of pride and adoration for myself. I took every compliment and added it to my bucket of self-centeredness, until Jesus sent that young man to humble me. This time I did not need him to.

When I grabbed the microphone on that day in church, tears were already forming in my heart and were making their way up to my face. I did everything I could think of to stop them from coming on stage, even to the point of not looking out at the crowd — not because I was too proud to cry in church (I've loaded up on Kleenex there a number of times), but because I wanted to finish the song. I had wasted my gift in bars and garages, and at drunken parties for too long. I wanted to sing for Him. I wanted to give something back to Him in appreciation for His gift. I wanted to make him proud.

"Praise the Lord, Sing to the Lord a new song, And His praise in the assembly of saints."
Psalms 149:1

Chapter 32

CHRISTIAN MUSIC?

Not all music being sold today as Christian music is Christian! You need to do your homework before listening to a particular band. If you don't, you might end up sorry in the long run.

The band U2 is often heralded as a "Christian" band, yet I am confused when I study their lyrics. In their 1987 song entitled "I Still Haven't Found What I'm Looking For" they sing the following:

> "You broke the bonds and you
> Loosed the chains
> Carried the cross
> Of my shame
> Of my shame
> You know I believed it
> But I still haven't found what I'm looking for . . ."
> [1]

Then on their 1997 album, they have a song called "MOFO" where they sing about looking for Jesus under the trash and use the f-word. In the very next song, they sing about God's angel. May I remind you that God is not the author of confusion. [2]

New Man magazine editor Bob Lipuaro inferred in his article "Solid Rock?" that "Christian" bands like P.O.D. are pushing the ideals that Bob Briner wrote of in his book *The Roaring Lambs* by "reshaping the moral climate." [3] Lipuaro should check back into reality. I believe without a doubt that P.O.D. is reshaping the moral climate, but not for the positive as his far-fetched dream has stated. Consider the following about P.O.D.

- After being asked by *Movieline* magazine, "Are you or are you not a Christian band?" they will answer: **"We're not,** but we do believe in Jesus." [4]

- You'll find them **cussing** in articles in the following magazines: *Guitar World*, (5) Rolling Stone, (6) *Circus*, (7) Drum, (8) Revolver, (9) and in the Associated Press. (10)

- You'll hear them admitting they used to smoke a lot of marijuana and stating, "Those were the best of times, **and I don't regret any of it**, because we had some fun." (11)

- You will read that when P.O.D. was asked if they drink beer, they responded: "**Of course we drink beer and we party.** You don't believe how often we get that question. People seem to have the misconception that we spend all our time on our knees praying, but I assure you, we don't. If there's a party, we party!" (12)

- You'll also find P.O.D. stating their theology in quotes such as, "It's not like Jesus is coming back." (13)

Lipuaro's article provides the following quote from novelist Stephen Bransford pertaining to a P.O.D. concert: "There were believers and unbelievers, mostly teens. Everybody got into the music, but it was the non-Christians who got it. I mean, they really understood what P.O.D. was doing. They were on the same wavelength." Well, I do not doubt it. P.O.D. is of the world and so are they. He said the Christians did not get it then, and obviously they still don't, or Lipuaro would not have written the article.

Lipuaro frequently called bands "musicians of faith." What faith? Faith in whom? Are they clear about who they have faith in? He called Run-DMC a band of faith from the past. Are you joking? Have you heard their remake of the Aerosmith song "Walk This Way?" It contains the following:

"Backstroke lover always hidin' 'neath the covers
"Gonna talk to you" my daddy say

Said "You ain't seen nothin' till you're down on a muffin
Then you're sure to be a changin' your ways". . .
Seesaw swingin' with the boys in school
And your feet flyin' up in the air
I sing "Hey diddle diddle"
Put your kitty in the middle of the swing
Like you didn't care." [14]

The band Creed is often promoted as a band of faith. Once again, a believer would have to take leave of their senses. Singer Scott Stapp blasphemes our Lord's name on their first album. This is the music that Christian magazines are promoting to the Christian youth of America?

Now, let us take a look at the so-called "Christian" band Lifehouse. When the UCLA *Daily Bruin* asked Lifehouse lead singer Jason Wade if they were a "Christian" band Wade stated, "We are not a 'Christian' band, but I'm a Christian . . . I don't feel that you have to label music as 'Christian' music. A Christian plumber is just a plumber." [15] Oh really! Okay, Wade, show me a plumber who stands in front of thousands of young people, and has an opportunity to share Christ with them, and then doesn't. Sounds like a great cop-out though.

When Wade was asked why he believes Lifehouse has had such a big following, he stated, "There's no explanation." [16] That's right, don't give the glory to God, because He has no part in their music. When asked about the group's lyrics, Wade answered, "That's the great thing about a song — a lyric may mean something totally different for someone else than it does for me and still be just as valid." [17] Well done, again, Wade. The songs you sing could talk about the cross, but no need to. Just let them mean whatever to whomever.

Who would Wade like to meet from the past that's no longer alive? John Lennon, [18] who had Aleister Crowley, a baby murderer, for a hero. When asked who his musical influences were, Wade cited the Beatles and Nirvana. [19] I need not say any more about The Beatles, but Nirvana, come on! Their lead singer, Kurt Cobain, committed suicide, and one of the group's album covers has the number "666" on it. Excellent influences? I think not. After you read this chapter, go to your local Bible bookstore. Chances, are Lifehouse and P.O.D. are on the shelf. Share this knowledge with the store's manager.

Also, don't forget that supposed "Christian" artists like Sixpence None The Richer and Jennifer Knapp are playing on the dreadful, anti-God Lilith Fair tour. Christians, this is a start for you, but do your homework and don't let the devil pull the wool over your eyes anymore.

1. http.//lyrics.interference.com/U2/lyrics
2. Ibid.
3. Bob Lipuaro "Solid Rock?" *New Man* (November/December 2002): 21.
4. "P.O.D. and the Works of Darkness," Dial-the-Truth Ministries, http://www.av1611.org/crock/pod_dark.html, 14.
5. *Guitar World* (Nov. 2001): 54, quoted in "P.O. D. and the Works of Darkness," Dial-the-Truth Ministries, http://www.av1611.org/crock/pod_dark.html, 14.
6. *Rolling Stone* (Nov. 22, 2001): 35, quoted in "P.O. D. and the Works of Darkness," Dial-the-Truth Ministries, http.//www.av1611.org/crock/pod_dark.html, 14.
7. *Circus* (July 2002): 22, quoted in "P.O.D. and the Works of Darkness," http://www.av1611.org/crock/pod_dark.html, 11,12.
8. *Drum!* (Sept.-Oct. 2001): 86-87, quoted in "P.O.D. and the Works of Darkness," Dial-the-Truth Ministries, http://www.av1611.org/crock/pod_dark.html, 11,12.
9. *Revolver* (Nov./Dec. 2001): 63, quoted in "P.O.D. and the Works of Darkness," Dial-the-Truth Ministries, http://www.av1611.org/crock/pod_dark.html, 12.
10. *Associated Press* (Nov. 2001): 59, quoted in "P.O.D. and the Works of Darkness," Dial-the-Truth Ministries, http://www.av1611.org/crock/pod_dark.html, 12.

11. *Revolver* (March/April 2002), quoted in "P.O.D. and the Works of Darkness," Dial-the-Truth Ministries, http://www.av1611.org/crock/pod_dark.html
12. *Circus* (July 2002): 22, quoted in "P.O.D. and the Works of Darkness," Dial-the-Truth Ministries, http://www.av1611.org/crock/pod_dark.html
13. *New Music* (June 2000): 45, quoted in "P.O.D. and the Works of Darkness," Dial-the-Truth Ministries, http://www.av1611.org/crock/pod_dark.html
14. http://letssingit.com
15. Http://www.dailybruin.ucla.edu/news/articles.asp?ID=2075
16. David, Wild, "The Rock & Roll Gospel According to Lifehouse" rollingstone.com, (June 07, 2001).
17. Jason Wade, Lifehouse: Play It Like It Is: Guitar (New York, New York: Cherry Lane Music Company, July 1, 2001), 5
18. Ibid
19. Ibid

Chapter 33

DON'T KID YOURSELF

Let us once again review Genesis, chapter 3, and that familiar scene in the garden. Verse one says that the serpent was more subtle then any beast of the field of which the Lord God had made. He used his cunning charm to lure Eve away from God. As I mentioned earlier, my pastor and I did a study of the word "subtle" in this particular text and found that it means "crafty" in a negative sense. The devil was slick with Eve and is still slick in his attempts to lead man astray today. The most crafty. The best deceiver. The best scammer. The best "player." The best liar. The most cunning beast of the field.

We have looked at some of the most sick and vile bands known to man. We have talked about their sinful lyrics, acts and lifestyles. We have seen how the devil himself has used these influences to lure man away from our Lord and Savior. But I want to remind you that the Bible says that satan is the most cunning beast of the field. And I want to show you that he is leading young people and adults of this world away from God by using some unlikely candidates also. He is using people and groups that many consider neutral, or good role models, or good ol' down-home Christians who are successful in the world today. Once again, it is time to peel the mask off the devil and expose him and his dirty deeds. Hang on to your hats, because this one is going to blow your mind.

I have heard a statement time and time again, since God put it in my heart to start this ministry. The voice says, "I know about those other bands, Mike, but I just listen to _____. They are neutral. They just sing about love and peace, and nonsense." If this is you, or you know someone like this, then this chapter is for you.

To solidify my point, let's regress and look at one more rock and roll band and its fruits.

The band is called Slipknot. Slipknot is a group of young men from Iowa who started up a rock band. They come from self-proclaimed "intact homes" and led ". . .

wholesome American lives." Yet their music takes on a very different outlook. Their guitarist, Mick Thompson, helps explain their demeanor: "I used to watch a lot of gore movies, lots of 'true death' videos. And at first, sure, I was disturbed by what I saw. But after a while, I became numb to it. With hard music, it's the same way. People listened to Korn, and now they want something even harder . . . it's like a drug." Enter Slipknot. [1]

In concert, the band has done the following things: They punch themselves and each other, they drink urine, they smear feces, they start fires and they throw up into the hideous masks they wear to cover up there faces. They write songs about stabbing people and then performing sex acts with the open wound. They are utterly sick and vile. Satan uses them to get to young people. Lead singer Shawn Craham states, "Every show, I've got some kid out there who's hitting himself just like me. His knuckles are bloody, his eyes black. I'll look into his eyes and see that he's in some other place. It's a heavy duty responsibility." [2]

An article in Detroit's *Metro Times* newspaper went into detail about the acts that the group performs, yet dismissed it all as youthful fun, and advised parents to allow their kids to attend Slipknot concerts without worries. [3] Slipknot, however, admits they are releasing the "poison" inside of them while spreading this message: "I hope they get a positive message for them, you know, that they don't have to answer to anything or anyone." Aleister Crowley's "do what thou wilt" rings out again. [4]

One mother stated not long ago in the news that she appreciated that her children were listening to the Backstreet Boys because they were supposedly focusing on good morals. Is she correct? 1 Thessalonians 5:22 says, "Prove all things; hold fast that which is good." [5] I have toured through the United States preaching, attended two years of Bible college, and worked on staff or with staff at five different churches in the last four years. One underlying commonality I have found is that the body of Christ is listening to rock music. I remember in one state, I preached at a youth rally about the dangers of popular music, and the altars were packed.

Afterwards, I was told by the hosting youth pastor that the biggest supporter of popular music in their church was the senior pastor.

I have seen people praising, dancing and worshiping God, yet still struggling and feeling defeated by the power of rock music in their lives. I have been to church services where Led Zeppelin songs were played in worship. (Remember, they are followers of Aleister Crowley.) I've been to services where they sang rock songs during worship service while spinning girls over their heads and flashing their bloomers. I have been to Christian weddings where rock music was played that openly opposed what the word of our God states. And it is far too typical to hear rock music blaring from the dorm rooms of Christian colleges and played on radios as people are pulling away from church.

If our youth are hearing God's word and music only a few hours a week, and listening to these "artists" preach all week long, who is most likely going to win the battle when it comes to crunch time? The devil. If the devil cannot take your soul to hell, he'll do the best he can to give you hell on earth. God's word says to "prove all things," so let's build a case. Going back to the mother's statement about the high morals of the Backstreet Boys, let's take a closer look at the band and its music. First, here are a few of the words to their song "Lay Down Beside Me":

> "I can't deny it
> The way your body swayed
> As I watched you from behind
> That got me so excited
> How could I fight it
> Baby let me be the one to hold you
> To give you the things I know you need . . .
> If you lay down, lay down beside me
> You can get all inside me
> And I can get all inside you too
> If you lay down, lay down beside me
> You can wake up beside me, forever." [6]

So what are they preaching to the youth of today? While the Bible tells us in 1 Corinthians 6:18 to "flee fornication," the all too frequent theme is to "do what thou wilt." One of the slang words for fornication is "lay." While many young people have screamed in protest that the band is talking about getting to know someone when they sing "lay down beside me," that theory is blown out of the water in the following lines:

> "Just come to me and get it,
> Baby, you won't regret it,
> I wanna feel your body next to mine,
> And before this night is over
> You will know what it means." (7)

In another song, "Boys Will Be Boys," the band sings of pressuring a girlfriend to accept their unwanted advances.

> "I try to get closer
> And you always push me away
> You tell me it's much too soon, but I just can't help it . . .
> All my senses go right into overdrive
> My defenses are never gonna hold,
> I'm always going to lose control
> I hear you saying
> That you think we should wait . . .
> My body's calling for you
> So please don't hesitate . . .
> I gotta do what I gotta do baby." (8)

And who is attending the Backstreet Boys concerts? *Entertainment Weekly* has this to say: "When Nick Carter — the youngest, blondest, and most yelp-inducing — blurts out the ludicrous line, 'Am I sexual?' hordes of 8- to 15 year-old girls clutch their throwaway camera and scream their braces off. Another night, another 10,000 sexual awakenings." (9)

Spin magazine states that when the boys sang the song "Everybody" — with the words 'Am I sexual?' the young girls pounded the stage so hard that roadies had to run to secure the speakers. The boys might be singing to teenage girls and boys, but they are not young themselves. Their ages are 29, 27, 26, 23, and 21. Yet the average age of their young fans at a "sexual awakening concert is 12 years old." (10)

Liz, one 15-year-old, described her fun night at a concert. She said that she walked to the front of the stage where a 12-year-old was standing on a crate, shoved the youngster off, ripped off her own bra and threw it to Nick of the Backstreet Boys. She then burst out crying and passed out. She stated that whenever she secs something new from the "Boys," she cries. (11)

The Backstreet Boys' A.J., who was recently in alcohol rehab, states ". . . I'm the opposite of every cleancut, decent looking guy you could think of." (12) He goes on to say that when he talks with women, he would rather be looking at their backsides then anything else. (13) These 20-something guys are singing to preteens and teens about expressing themselves sexually. In their song "I Need You Tonight," they sing "I need you tonight ... And I know deep within my heart, it doesn't matter if it's wrong or right." How many fathers would want these 20-something-year-old guys singing to their teenage daughters on the phone? Yet it is happening through CD players across America, inside and outside of the church. (14)

The last Backstreet Boys' song that I want to talk about is "If You Want It to Be Good (Get Yourself a Bad Boy)." The song repeats the title words several times and follows with the line, "And Momma shouldn't know." So much for their good morals. (15)

Although the band sings about sex all night and appeared on the cover of *Rolling Stone* magazine with their pants dropped down to their knees, they start each concert night with a ritual prayer. With the words these men sing and the sexual awakenings that they stir, they are not going to receive God's blessing on their concerts. Psalms 66:18 states, "If I regard iniquity in my heart, the Lord will not hear me." Yet the band has **someone's** anointing. They sold 1.13 million copies of their record in the first week, shattering records that the music industry thought were unbreakable. (16)

Let us look at another band. It is called 'N SYNC. 'N SYNC's album *No Strings Attached* absolutely shattered the Backstreet Boys' record by selling 2.41 million copies in the first week. *TV Guide* describes the song "Digital Get Down" (a song from the previously mentioned album) as "R-rated oomph" and says, "Digital Get Down" could be interpreted as hailing the joys of cybersex." [17]

The following are a few lines from the song:

> "Baby, baby we can do all that we want
> We're gettin' nasty, we're getting freaky, freaky
> Baby, baby, we can do more then just talk . . .
> If you're in the mood and on the phone . . .
> I can't wait to see you touch your body, girl." [18]

With the number of perverts and pedophiles that already populate the Internet, all we need is for a rock group to encourage the youth of America to participate in phone sex. When *TV Guide* asked lead singer Justin Timberlake about the obvious content of the song, he said, "I think it's quite safe sex if you ask me." [19]

Without going into more detail, several of 'N SYNC's other songs make obvious references to having sex. As Timberlake was recording one of their hit songs, producer Guy Riche stated, "It's a hit already. I see panties flying." [20] He was referring to the fans that remove their bras and panties and throw them onstage at Backstreet Boys and 'N SYNC concerts.

Any guesses who 'N SYNC takes time to thank on their album? They thank God and the Lord Jesus Christ. Ultraliberal *Rolling Stone* magazine calls 'N SYNC's music "darker stuff, like teen horror movies and grunge" and they go on to say it's ". . . brimming with pent-up tension of teenhood: the urgency of unfulfilled, misunderstood desires, burbling hormones and unbearable, overwhelming feelings." [21] If that is what liberal *Rolling Stone* thinks, what should we, as Christians, think?

The next artist I want to look at is Timberlake's former live-in girlfriend, Britney Spears. Britney has openly stated that she is a Baptist Christian. In Matthew 7:16-20, the Bible tells us that we will know them by their fruits. So let us evaluate her fruit, or lack thereof.

We will take a look at her lyrics, but first I want to review her photo history and interviews. Consider the photo shoot that Spears did for *Rolling Stone* magazine. *Iowa State Daily* describes her cover photo as "a barely-clad Spears wearing little more than a bra and a smile." [22]

The article itself is called "Britney Spears: Inside the Heart, Mind & Bedroom of a Teen Dream." In the article, Britney appears in her underwear and high heels, with her little girl dolls on the shelf behind her. In another photo, she is standing with a little girl's pink bike and the word "Baby" written across the backside of her extremely short shorts. [23] An Internet news page (MSN) article described the photos as a "pedophile's dream." [24] When asked by MTV about the photos, Spears answered, "I think it's fine and it's tasteful." [25]

At the American Music Awards, Spears' her attire was unbelievable. One viewer stated, "She may as well have come naked to the awards show." She wore what one person described as a "backless dress worn backwards." John Bream of the *Minneapolis Star Tribune* said, "I'm no prude, but that isn't the kind of outfit someone who has a big influence on young people should be wearing on prime-time TV. This kind of racy/sexy/trashy ensemble is what music followers might expect from Carmen Electra, Pamela Anderson Lee, or Mariah Carey." [26]

Then Spears went to the MTV Music Awards. One reporter from liberal music station VH-1 said, "Britney Spears provided some medieval thrills by hanging, drawing, and then quartering the Rolling Stones' 'I Can't Get No Satisfaction' in a transparent body stocking. For a few brief moments, it was as if child pornography had gone overground." [27] Comedian and MTV host Marlon Wayans remarked as Spears shed her clothing, "She's gone from the Mickey Mouse Club to the strip club!" [28] Her attire was so outrageous that even her 22-year-old brother Bryan told *People* magazine, "Lately I've been telling her she needs to put on more clothes instead of some of the outfits she ends up wearing." [29]

Spears posed topless for the front cover of the August 18, 2003 issue of *Elle* magazine. She then posed topless for the September 30, 2003 issue of *Rolling Stone* magazine. Spears also appeared on the front cover of *Esquire* magazine's October 3, 2003 issue. In that photo, she is wearing a long sweater that covers the front portion of her body, yet she is standing sideways, with her bare buttocks clearly shown for the camera view. [30]

In an interview with *Elle*, Spears stated she says her prayers at night, but that she also freely employs the f-word. She then admitted she is addicted to the sexually explicit *Sex and the City* TV show. She goes on to talk about the show by saying, "Like one show was talking about how guys can have sex without love, so women can do it too. And I have girlfriends who do that. But I just really have to be into someone. If not, what's the purpose." [31]

As far as her song lyrics go, *Entertainment Weekly* described her music as "perversely inspired and sexually ambiguous." [32] They are correct. In Spears recent album she sings a song called "Touch of My Hand." She revealed in a recent *People* magazine article that the song is an ode to masturbation. She stated, "I think it's a positive thing to indulge in yourself in a sexual way sometimes. I don't do it all the time. It's life ... It's a positive thing." She goes on, "When you turn yourself on, that really is what turns the guy on. So just make yourself happy and let them just kind of follow up after you." [33]

To finish up this section on Spears, she has had surgery to enlarge her breast size, had her videos directed by pornography director Gregory Dark, and wrote her own movie script, which features her in two sex scenes. Yet Spears is always happy to proclaim her Christian faith and then later admit she is emulating her hero, Madonna. [34] Madonna. Does this ring a bell? Britney Spears open-mouthed kissed Madonna, her idol, at the opening for a MTV Music Awards ceremony. [35] This behavior is now being copied by young girls across our nation. This is hardly a statement for God.

Well, in looking at Spears' fruit, we should look at modesty. 1 Timothy 2:9 reads, "In like manner also, that women adorn themselves in modest apparel . . ." We should look at her company — meaning her producers, friends and ex-boyfriend. Amos 3:3 reads, "Can two walk together, except they be agreed?" Regarding her actions, we should look at 1 Corinthians 6:18, which again states, "flee fornication." If we return to Matthew 7:16-20, it would appear Spears is a wolf in sheep's clothing.

What is the underlying element in all of this music? The answer is sex! Sex that is outside of the bonds of holy matrimony!!! We all know too well the amount of sex that is shown and talked about in movies, teen shows, books, magazines and commercials. But what about in music? Music is such a subtle tool (the most subtle beast of the field) to indoctrinate thoughts. Music is played at home, in cars, in stores, in schools, in churches, etc. And the most common theme is sex. As long as groups are not singing about the devil, or drugs, or violence, or alcohol, it is far too easily passed off as neutral music.

It is taught in schools and accepted by millions that young people will have sex before marriage, and our pathetic prayers are to hope it is not often, with few partners, and that they use some form of protection. Yet the Bible states that sex before marriage is fornication. Just like the world is now desensitized to school shootings, it was desensitized long before to the fact that young people and adults will participate in sex before marriage. And the "neutral" music takes a big part in pushing them along.

Now that we have looked at pop bands in great detail, let's take a look at a few country, rhythm and blues, and rap bands to see if the same principle – that satan is influencing the music — applies to other genres. We'll start with country.

The lyrics to country singer Alan Jackson's song "Where Were You When the World Stopped Turning?" read:

> "But I know Jesus and I talk to God
> And I remember this from when I was young
> Faith, hope and love are some good things He gave us and the greatest is love." [36]

Yet he also is happy to sing the song "I Don't Need the Booze to Get a Buzz on," which goes as follows:

> "I've been known to tie one on and honky tonk til past three
> But the party don't get started til my baby pours her love on me
> She's a hundred proof, Lord she's smooth
> She makes me moan all night long
> So I don't need the booze to get a buzz on." (37)

Country singer Toby Keith sings "Jesus Gets Jealous of Santa Claus" with the words:

> "So, with her head on my shoulder
> And her tears mixed with mine
> I thought how little baby Jesus
> Gets left out at Christmas time
> It ain't about the money
> Oh, money can't buy love
> And I saw the light that Christmas night
> With help from up above." (38)

But his new smash single is called "I'm Just Talkin' About Tonight," with the following lyrics:

> "I'm not talkin' 'bout locking down forever, baby
> That would be too demanding
> I'm just talkin' 'bout two lonely people
> who might reach a little understanding
> I'm not talkin' 'bout knocking out heaven
> with whether we're wrong or we're right
> I'm not talkin' 'bout hooking up or hanging out
> I'm just talkin' 'bout tonight." (39)

Then there are the Dixie Chicks. In their song called "Sin Wagon" they poke fun at an old gospel favorite:

> "On a mission to make something happen
> Feel like Delilah lookin' for Sampson
> Do a little mattress dancin'
> That's right I said mattress dancin'

> Praise the Lord and pass the ammunition
> Need a little bit more
> of what I have been missin'
> I don't know where I'll be crashin'
> But I'm arrivin' on a sin wagon . . . **I'll fly away**
> on a sin wagon." (40) (emphasis mine)

As far as rap groups go, I was hard-pressed to find some lyrics that are repeatable. But here are a few. Previously we talked about the Baha Men and their song "Who Let The Dogs Out?" May I remind you it is not about someone leaving the backdoor to the house open. It is about a man and women having sex in a particular position. And there is the Bloodhound Gang, with their song that appeals to the young generation, called "The Bad Touch":

> "So show me yours, I'll show you mine *Tool Time*
> you'll Lovett just like Lyle
> And then we'll do it doggy-style so we can both watch *X-Files* . . .
> You and me baby ain't nothin' but mammals
> So let's do it like they do on the Discovery Channel. " (41)

The video shows them dressed as dogs and humping each other. Then they show a drug-induced rape. The song sold platinum. And we wonder where young people get their ideas. C'mon, Christians, wake up!!!

As far as the state of rap, Luther Campbell and 2 Live Crew set the tone in 1988 with their album *As Nasty as They Wanna Be*. It contained "226 uses of the f-word, 117 explicit terms for male and female genitalia, 87 descriptions of oral sex, 81 uses of the vulgarity sh-t, 4 descriptions of group sex, 2 inclusions of urination and feces, 9 descriptions of ejaculation" and much more. (42) Without further discussion, I can assure you that rap music has not gotten better. It should be noted though that liberal *48 Hours* host Dan Rather cried, "censorship," when a judge declared this album obscene. (43)

Pop rock superstar and gospel singer Whitney Houston's lyrics in "Saving All My Love for You" find pleasure in adultery: "A few stolen moments, is all that we share. You've got your family, and they need you there. Though I try to resist being last on your list . . . So I'm saving all my love for you. We'll be making love the whole night through." [44] To make matters worse, the world will take these stars who have made absolute millions by educating America about sex, drugs, and hedonistic lifestyles, and turn them into heroes for singing one love song or raising money for charity. The following are examples.

Rhythm and Blues star R. Kelly (who thanks God for his success) sings about his enjoyment of promiscuity all the time, and then becomes a hero when he writes a song to raise money for AIDS research, which is a disease widely spread because of promiscuity. [45]

Pop singer Elton John is made a national hero when he writes a song about the late princess Diana, yet makes the statement, "There's nothing wrong with people going to bed with someone of your own sex. I just think people should be very free with sex . . . They should draw the line at goats." [46]

Janet Jackson, who is often considered one of the good guys (and also thanks God for her musical success), on her Velvet Rope tour raised money to mentor children in disadvantaged circumstances with the help of our national leader, General Colin Powell. Poverty, poor self-esteem, broken homes and disease are often the results of sexual promiscuity. Yet Jackson's songs and tours refer to genital piercing, bondage scenes, sex outside of marriage and partial nudity. [47]

For Jackson's video, entitled "If," "close to 80 pregnant 13- to 17-year-olds, or teens that recently had babies, were invited down (to watch the shooting) by Jackson." There was one individual, though, who was discouraged from dropping by — Katherine Jackson (her mom). "The one person that kept running through my head while I was writing these songs was my mother," Jackson says. "(I told her) 'Some of my movements are very sexy . . . I'd be embarrassed if you were there.'" [48] The video shows Jackson abusing a male dancer, rubbing her hands over his entire body, and several simulations of the two of them having sex.

In Luke 16:15, Jesus said, "You are those that justify yourselves before men, but God knows your hearts. For what is highly esteemed among men is an abomination in the sight of God." Why would any God-fearing Christian want to listen to any of these songs or artists? My answer is that I have absolutely no idea. Ephesians 5:8-12 tells us, "For you were once darkness, but now you are light in the Lord. Walk as children of light (for the fruit of the Spirit is in all goodness, righteousness, and truth), finding out what is acceptable to the Lord. And have no fellowship with the unfruitful works of darkness, but rather expose them. For it is shameful even to speak of those things which are done by them in secret."

Who do these bands and others target today? They target teens. Teenagers are impressionable. We all know this is the time when young peoples' bodies begin to form and change, and they began to pay more attention to the opposite sex. They start to grow into the man or woman that they will soon become. The choices that young people make in their teen years will affect them for the rest of their lives. As a police officer, I arrested several young people and watched as their choices sent them off to jail. As a counselor, I listened and prayed as I was told of 12-, 13- and 14-year-old girls having sex before their little bodies had even developed. As a street minister, I listened to ex-cons, drug addicts and drunks cry out in despair over the choices they had made as adolescents.

I myself deal with repercussions on a daily basis for choices I made in my younger days. Now make no mistake about it, God has forgiven me and restored me, but I still reap repercussions. Nothing, absolutely nothing had a greater influence on my life in those days than my music. It was my Bible, and little did I know it, but satan was my god.

The Bible tells us in 2 Timothy 2:22 to "flee also youthful lusts." Youth have problems fleeing lusts, especially when they see adults embracing their own. I have spoken with countless men who struggle with their need to view pornography and indulge in their lusts of the flesh, and one common factor among them is the movies and TV programs that they watch, the magazines they read, and the music that they listen to. The devil is no dummy.

As the evidence has shown, there is an alarming amount of sexual material in the pop music genre. Sadly, it does not stop short of taking an all out swing at God and His word either. It used to be somewhat subtle, with songs such as "Jacob's Ladder" by Huey Lewis, which illustrates his selfish ambition:

> "She was running from a fat man
> Selling salvation in his hand.
> Now he's trying to save me,
> Well I'm doing alright, the best that I can.
> Just another fallen angel . . ." [49]

One also can see the idolatry in Van Halen's "Best of Both Worlds" when they sing:

> "You don't have to die to go to heaven
> Or hang around to be born again.
> Just tune in to what this place has got to offer,
> 'Cause we may never be here again." [50]

One of the most notable anti-Bible campaigns is a tour sponsored by Sara McLachlan called Lilith Fair. Lilith is the mythical creature noted as Adam's first wife. She supposedly had enough of Adam and God, and the fact that she was to submit to both of them, and walked out of the Garden of Eden in rebellion, leaving them behind. This tour is humongous, with big name acts such as the following performing:

> Christina Aguilera
> Suzanne Vega
> The Pretenders
> Liz Phair
> Meshell Ndegeocello
> Mya
> Monica
> Sara McLachlan

Martina McBride
Luscious Jackson
Lisa Loeb
Queen Latifah
Indigo Girls
Dixie Chicks
Sheryl Crow
Deborah Cox
Shawn Colvin
Sandra Bernhard

These supposedly Christian artists have also appeared:

Jennifer Knapp and Sixpence None The Richer [51]

Sara McLachlan ends her song "Dear God" with the following:

"Dear God,
Don't know if you noticed, but . . .
Your name is on a lot of quotes on this book,
Us crazy humans wrote it, you should take a look,
And all the people that you made in your image,
Still believing that junk is true
Well I know it ain't, and so do you
Dear God,
I can't believe in . . .
I don't believe in . . .
I won't believe in heaven and hell.
No saints, no sinners, no devil as well.
No pearly gates, no thorny crown.
You're always letting us humans down.
The wars you bring, the babes you drown.
Those lost at sea and never found
And it's the same the whole world 'round,
The hurt I see helps to compound
The Father, Son, and Holy Ghost
Is just somebody's unholy hoax
And if you're up there you'd perceive
That my heart's here upon my sleeve.
It there's one thing I don't believe in . . .

It's you." (52)

To close out this chapter, I want to look at some evidence that absolutely turns my stomach. The following people give the glory to God for their outright sin and debauchery. They thanked Jesus Christ and/or God for their music awards:

> Whitney Houston
> Destiny's Child
> Christina Aguilera
> 'N SYNC
> Sisqó (who attributes his success to Jesus and women's thong underwear)
> Britney Spears
> Lenny Kravitz (who depicts numerous sex scenes in his videos)
> Janet Jackson
> Salt and Peppa
> Jessica Simpson
> Backstreet Boys
> Missy Elliot (whose music is full of cuss words)
> Moby (who thinks nothing of it to date strippers and prostitutes and perform naked)
> Puff Daddy
> R. Kelly
> Toni Braxton
> and Mariah Carey, to name a few. (53)

2 Peter 2:1,2,3,6,10,12,13,14,17,18,19 states:

> Sometimes false prophets spoke to the people of Israel, false teachers will also sneak in and speak harmful lies to you. But these teachers don't really belong to the Master who paid a great price for them, and they will quickly destroy themselves. Many people will follow their evil ways and cause others to tell lies about the true way. They will be greedy and cheat you with smooth talk. But long ago God decided to punish them, and God doesn't sleep. God punished the cities of Sodom and Gomorrah by burning them to ashes,

and this is a warning to anyone else that wants to sin. The Lord is especially hard on people who disobey Him and don't think of anything except their own filthy desires. They are reckless and proud and are not afraid of cursing the glorious beings in heaven. These people are no better then senseless animals that live by their feelings and are born to be bought and killed. They speak evil of things they don't know anything about. But their own corrupt deeds will destroy them. They have done evil and will be rewarded with evil. They think it is fun to have wild parties during the day ... All they think about is having sex with someone else's husband or wife. There is no end to their wicked deeds. They trick people who are easily fooled, and their minds are filled with greedy thoughts. But they are headed for trouble. The darkest part of hell is waiting for them. They brag out loud about their stupid nonsense. And by being vulgar and crude, they trap people who have barely escaped from living the wrong kind of life. They promise freedom to everyone. But they are merely slaves of filthy living, because people are slaves of whatever controls them. (54)

Proverbs 13:20 reads, "He who walks with wise men shall be wise, but a companion of fools shall be destroyed." (NIV) It is extremely important who man associates with, what he listens to, and whom he imitates, lest he be destroyed. Just because someone makes a gospel album should not be enough for us to throw them in the mix as a Christian singer. If this is the only requirement then I will be happy to sell you Charles Manson's greatest gospel hits.

As we close, let us reflect on Joshua 24:15. It states, "And if it seems evil to you to serve the Lord, choose for yourselves this day whom you will serve, whether the gods which your fathers served . . . But as for me and my house, we will serve the Lord." There has been more than enough information and biblical proof in this book to show you that God does not want you to listen to "popular" music. You now have the knowledge. If you still choose to listen and think God's stance is unfair, then it must "seem evil to you to serve the Lord."

For me, and countless people I have spoken to, this information has been enough to quit. God does not play games. If you do a study on the word "house" as is written in Joshua 24:15, you will find that it means more then just the structure. When Joshua said "my house," that included his family and the things in the house. In modern day, this would include your television, radio, CD player, magazine collection, etc. Joshua said everything in his house will serve the Lord, and it should not be any different in our houses today.

God wants us to serve Him with righteousness and holiness. I know it might not be easy in the beginning, but He will give you the strength. Call on your pastor. Tell him of your struggle, and ask him to pray with you. Confess your struggles to your friends and tell them you need their prayers. Ask other Christians what Christian music they listen to, or go to your Bible bookstore and ask for help. Remember though, to beware. There are bands posing as Christian that do not bear the fruit of a true brother or sister.

Above all, call on God. Always remember to run to the throne before you run to the phone. Ask God for forgiveness for your rebellion. Thank Him for this book and for putting it in your hands. Ask Him to deliver you from this addiction and to give you strength and wisdom.

I love you my brother and sister and I am praying for you. God did it for me, and I know He will do it for you too. Spread the Word!!!

---

1. *Guitar World* (June 2000): 9, quoted in Holmberg, *Hell's Bells 2*, video.
2. *Rolling Stone* (May 6-20, 2000): 76, quoted in Holmberg, *Hell's Bells 2*, video.
3. Nicole Jones, *Metro Times* (Oct.31-Nov. 6, 2001): 21.
4. *Rolling Stone* (May 6-20, 2000) 76, quoted in Holmberg, *Hell's Bells 2*, video.
5. Max Lucado, *The Inspirational Study Bible: New King James Version of the Bible*, (Dallas, Texas: Thomas Nelson, Inc., 1982.)
6. Terry Watkins, "The Dirty Little Secret about Rock's Teen Idols: What are The Backstreet Boys, N'Sync & Britney Spears really

saying?" Dial-the-Truth Ministries, http://www.av1611.org/othpubls/teenidol.html, 3.
7. Ibid.
8. Watkins, "The Dirty Little Secret about Rock's Teen Idols, 4
9. Ibid.
10. Author Name, "In Bed With...the Backstreet Boys," *Spin* (July 1998): http://www.geocities.com/SunsetStrip/Balcony/1828/spin.htm, quoted in Terry Watkins, "The Dirty Little Secret about Rock's Teen Idols: What are The Backstreet Boys, N'Sync & Britney Spears really saying?" Dial-the-Truth Ministries, http://www.av1611.org/othpubls/tccnidol.html, 3.
11. Ibid.
12. Author, "The Boys are Back," *Teen* (July 1999): Terry Watkins, "The Dirty Little Secret about Rock's Teen Idols: What are The Backstreet Boys, N'Sync & Britney Spears really saying?" Dial-the-Truth Ministries, http://www.av1611.org/othpubls/teenidol.html, 3.
13. Watkins, "The Dirty Little Secret about Rock's Teen Idols, 5.
14. Ibid.
15. Ibid.
16. Watkins, "The Dirty Little Secret about Rock's Teen Idols, 6.
17. *TV Guide* (April 1, 2000): 26 Terry Watkins, "The Dirty Little Secret about Rock's Teen Idols: What are The Backstreet Boys, N'Sync & Britney Spears really saying?" Dial-the-Truth Ministries, http://www.av1611.org/othpubls/teenidol.html, 3.
18. Watkins, "The Dirty Little Secret about Rock's Teen Idols, 7.
19. *TV Guide* (April 1, 2000): 26, Terry Watkins, "The Dirty Little Secret about Rock's Teen Idols: What are The Backstreet Boys, N'Sync & Britney Spears really saying?" Dial-the-Truth Ministries, http://www.av1611.org/othpubls/teenidol.html, 3.
20. *Entertainment Weekly* (March 5, 1999): 20 Terry Watkins, "The Dirty Little Secret about Rock's Teen Idols: What are The Backstreet Boys, N'Sync & Britney Spears really saying?" Dial-the-Truth Ministries, http://www.av1611.org/othpubls/teenidol.html, 3.
21. *Rolling Stone* (March 30, 2000): 55 Terry Watkins, "The Dirty Little Secret about Rock's Teen Idols: What are The Backstreet Boys, N'Sync & Britney Spears really saying?" Dial-the-Truth Ministries, http://www.av1611.org/othpubls/teenidol.html, 3.
22. *Iowa State Daily* (April 5, 1999): page number, quoted in Watkins, "The Dirty Little Secret about Rock's Teen Idols, 10.
23. "Article?" *Rolling Stone*, (April 15, 1999): quoted in Watkins, "The Dirty Little Secret about Rock's Teen Idols, 10.
24. Carla A. DeSantis, "Exploit Me, Baby, One More Time,"MSN, quoted in Watkins, "The Dirty Little Secret about Rock's Teen Idols, 10.
25. http://www.wallofsound.go.com/archive/news/stories/britney041499.html

26. Jon Bream, "Wishin' and Hopin': Planting the Seeds of Change for a Better Music World in 2000," *Minneapolis Star Tribune* (Jan.1, 2000): 5F, quoted in Watkins, "The Dirty Little Secret about Rock's Teen Idols."
27. C. Bottomley, "MTV Awards: Where Are Bone Thugs-N-Harmony When You Need Them," www.vh1.com, quoted in Watkins, "The Dirty Little Secret about Rock's Teen Idols."
28. Watkins, "The Dirty Little Secret about Rock's Teen Idols, 12.
29. Author, "Britney's Wild Ride," People.com (Feb. 14, 2000). http://people.aol.com/people/000214/features/index.html, quoted in Watkins, "The Dirty Little Secret about Rock's Teen Idols, 12.
30. www.linkoregon.com/britney-spears-2.htm.
31. *Elle* (Oct. 2000): 331, Terry Watkins, "The Dirty Little Secret about Rock's Teen Idols: What are The Backstreet Boys, N'Sync & Britney Spears really saying?" Dial-the-Truth Ministries, http://www.av1611.org/othpubls/teenidol.html, 12.
32. *Entertainment Weekly* (May 19, 2000): 71, quoted in Watkins, "The Dirty Little Secret about Rock's Teen Idols.
33. Watkins, "The Dirty Little Secret about Rock's Teen Idols,13.
34. http://www.nydailynews.com/front/story/13603p-121256c.html
35. http://www.sing365.com
36. Ibid.
37. www.linkoregon.com/britney-spears-2.htm
38. http://www.sing365.com
39. Ibid.
40. http://www.geocities.com
41. Ibid.
42. http://www.family.org/docstudy/solid/a0014931.html
43. Ibid.
44. Steven Peters, *Truth About Rock* (Minneapolis: Bethany House, 1998), 32.
45. Eric Holmberg, *Hell's Bells 2: The Dangers of Rock 'n' Roll*, 2001, Reel 2 Real Ministries, video.
46. Peters, *Truth About Rock*, 39.
47. Holmberg, *Hell's Bells 2,* video.
48. *Us Weekly* (Aug. 1993): 74-92 quoted in Holmberg, Hell's Bells 2, video.
49. http://www.lyricsxp.com
50. http://www.geocities.com
51. http://www.lilithfair.com/artists/index.html
52. http:/www.lyricattack.com
53. Holmberg, *Hell's Bells 2*, video.
54. *New Testament, Psalms and Proverbs, Contemporary English Version of the Bible* (New York: American Bible Society, 1995).

Chapter 34

GUILTY

Guilty. Guilty. Guilty. There is no other verdict. He did it and he is still doing it. Satan led Eve astray in the garden and he is leading God's children astray yet today. He told Eve in Genesis 3:5, "you will be like God" if you follow your own will. And today he is telling the body of Christ that "they can be like God" and still do things according to their own will, without consequence.

Well, he lied. That's no big surprise. The Bible calls him the "father of lies" in John 8:44. There are consequences for sin, just as Eve and Adam found out soon after eating the fruit. They wanted to serve God and yet follow their own will. My friends, that is impossible. There is only one way, and it's God's way.

Remember, you're the jury, and the following is my closing argument. Let's consider three issues. "Does the devil have the means to commit the crime?" "Was satan at the scene of the crime?" Third, and possibly most importantly, "Does the devil have a motive to commit the crime?"

Question 1: "Does the devil have the means to commit the crime?"

>Let's look once again at Ezekiel 28:13. It reads "The workmanship of thy tabrets and of thy pipes was prepared in thee in the day that thou wast created." If you look up "tabrets" in *Strong's Exhaustive Concordance of the Bible,* you will find that it means "tambourines." Tambourines were very common musical instruments in Old Testament times and still are today. Lucifer (satan), in his pre-fallen state, had tambourines created by God inside of him. He had music emanating from his body, and as we established in chapter 3, Lucifer had a creative anointing to emanate beautiful music. So does he have the means to commit the crime? Without any doubt, satan has the ability to create music.

(Side note: If you read Ezekiel 28:13 and find a verse that seems very different than the one I have shown, I challenge you to look at the original translation. Check the *King James Bible* and the *New King James Bible*, which are translated from the original version.)

Question 2: Was satan at the scene of the crime?

> Once again, yes. Most likely you were amazed to find out about Aleister Crowley. He was, without a doubt, a follower of satan. He set out to destroy Christianity by spreading the theme "Do what thou wilt." He spread it to Kenneth Anger, Timothy Leary, Anton LaVey and Hezekiah Ben Aaron. Remember, Crowley stated he received the message from a "shadowy presence." It was no angel. It was satan, or one of his demons, as it was the same lie told to Eve in the garden.
>
> Do not forget the quotes from the musicians themselves. Carlos Santana claims he received his music from Metatron. We spoke in chapter 20 of how Metatron was directly tied in with Crowley. We read quotes from Alanis Morissette, John Lennon, Robert Palmer, Tony Iommi and others, of how the music just came to them or was channeled through them. We read how Angus Young, John McLaughlin, Peter DiStefano and Ozzy Osbourne stated that some outside force was performing through them. And we also heard Jimi Hendrix's girlfriend, Faye Prigdon, state that Hendrix had a demon, or devil, within him and "songs and different things like that just came out of him." That was not God speaking to Aleister Crowley, and believe me, it was not the holy God of heaven leading these artists either. It, again, was satan. Was he at the scene of the crime? Obviously, and he left clues everywhere.

Question 3: Does the devil have a motive to commit the crime?

> Yes. Yes. Yes. What does satan want? He wants your soul! He wants you to spend eternity with him in hell. The Bible is very clear about the fact that some men and women will go to hell. Satan is trying to take as many of you with him as he can. Revelation 21:8 states, "But the fearful and unbelieving, and the abominable, and murderers, and whoremongers, and sorcerers, and idolaters, and all liars, shall have their part in the lake which burneth with fire and brimstone."
>
> If we again return to *Strong's Exhaustive Concordance of the Bible*, we will find the following definitions. In this verse, "fearful" means faithless, "unbelieving" means a heathen, "abominable" means to disgust God, especially with idolatry. "Murderer" means one who intentionally takes another life with criminal intent, "whoremonger" means fornicator, "sorcerer" means one who distributes drugs and/or a magician, "idolater" means an image worshiper, and a "liar" means one who is deceitful and/or wicked.

What does popular music as a whole preach? It preaches fornication, use of drugs (remember alcohol is a drug), anger and/or murder, and embracing a "heathen" lifestyle. The Bible specifically states that one who participates in these and then does not receive the forgiveness of God will enter the lake of fire. The Bible states in Matthew 5:21-22 that those who anger against their brother without cause are in danger of judgment. Jesus then tells you to make peace with your adversary quickly. Matthew 5:28 reads, "Whoever looks at a woman to lust for her has already committed adultery with her in his heart." Jesus then warns we can be cast into hell for this also. It is not only our actions, but our thoughts that can lead us to hell. Let's not forget idolatry. Entertainers in this day and age have become idols. We all know that people young and old worship them. May I remind you that each one of them is just a human like you and me, except that they live in the spotlight. On a whole, our entertainers are morally bankrupt, yet they are American idols.

Well, satan has the means, he was at the scene, and he has the motive. We have found his fingerprints (clues) everywhere. And now I provide the "smoking gun." As the last witness, I call myself.

Popular music is a lie, and that lie almost took me to the lake of fire. I bought it, I listened to it, and I loved it, probably to much more of an extent then most of you, but all it takes it a little leaven. God walked me through my life in this book, and it scared me. I am very well aware that as you sit in your car, office, home, etc. tonight, I, Michael Plont, could be writhing in torment in hell. But God spared me. He sent Sylvia Rogers into my life to warn me of the hell that awaited me, and I can tell you, the very first thing she told me was if I did not give up this music, I was headed for hell. She was right.

If I returned to listening to popular music, satan would again become part of my life. I would slowly and subtly slide back into a life of hedonism, just like the frog in the pot on the stove. If you turn up the heat, he will instantly jump out. But if you increase the heat slowly, he will just lie there and let you cook him. That's the way it is with this music, satan will slowly roast your soul.

God has called me to be a watchdog for the body of Christ, so here is your warning — Turn off the rock music and leave it off. Johann Sebastian Bach said it best when he commented, "The end of all music should be the glory of God and the refreshment of the human spirit."

As I close this book, my friend, I want to thank you for taking the time to read it. It is my hope that you are convinced by the overwhelming evidence that has been presented that the devil is responsible for the state of popular music. And it is my greater hope that you will want to be free from the hold this music has on your life. I would like to pray that first, you would give your life to Christ, who died for you, and second, that you could be free from this music forever.

It is a misconception that you have to clean up your life and then go to a church to give your life to Christ. I was far from God the day I gave my life to Him, and it is exactly why I wanted to do so. My life with Christ started with a simple prayer like this:

> Jesus, I know that you are the Son of God, and I know You came to Earth and died for my sins, and then three days later rose from the dead. I know I am a sinner, and I am asking You to come into my life, and wash me with your blood, and be my Lord and Savior forever. In Jesus's name I pray, Amen.

After my eyes were opened, and I realized the truth about popular music, I said a prayer like the following:

> Lord, I thank you for showing me the truth about today's music. I realize the stronghold it has had on my life and mind, and I no longer wish to be controlled by it. I am asking You to set me free and to wash me clean with the blood You shed on the cross. God please put music in my life that honors Your name, so I can be changed. In Jesus's name I pray, Amen.

My friend, God will honor your prayer. He will save you and He will set you free. I recommend you get plugged into a church that glorifies Jesus and follows His Bible. There is a church out there for you, so find one where you feel "alive" and let the Lord change your life. I love you, I am praying for you, and don't you ever give up on God.

INDEX

-A-
AC/DC – 12, 32, 34, 50, 58, 75, 80, 114
Acts 7:9-10a – 107
Aguilera, Christina – 136, 138
Amos, Tori – 78, 88

-B-
Backstreet Boys – 124-128, 138, 140, 141
Baha Men – 75, 133
Beatles – 28-30, 42-44, 46, 56, 77, 83, 120
Black Crowes – 23
Black Sabbath – 56, 66, 77
Bloodhound Gang – 133
Blue Oyster Cult – 56
Bowie, David – 23, 84

-C-
Cinderella – 106
1 Corinthians 6:18 – 131
2 Corinthians 2:11 – 49
2 Corinthians 4:4,6 – 16, 114
2 Corinthians 6:14 – 80

-D-
Daniel 5:4,30 – 70
Def Leppard – 99
Deuteronomy 13:1-5 – 80
Divinyls – 34
Dixie Chicks – 132, 137
Doors, The – 36, 37

-E-
Ephesians 2:2 – 16
Ezekiel 28:13 – 73, 78, 143, 144
Exodus 20:3 – 26

-F-
Fox, Samantha – 34
Freed, Alan – 71

-G-

Galatians 5:19,21 - 54
Galatians 6:7,8 - 76, 109
Genesis 2:18 - 100
Genesis 3:1,5 - 16, 123, 143
Guns N' Roses - 102, 103

-H-
Hagar, Sammy - 25, 26, 51
Hall, Darryl - 24
Hendrix, Jimi - 42, 81, 82, 89, 144
Houston, Whitney - 134, 138

-I-
Isaiah 57:3,4 - 29

-J-
Jackson, Alan - 131
Jackson, Janet - 134
Jackson, Michael - 76, 79, 88
James 1:14 - 12, 35
James 3:13-17 - 76
James 4:4 - 61
John 3:16 - 112
John, Elton - 134
1 John 2:17 - 62

-K-
Keith, Toby - 132
Kelly, R. - 134, 138
Kiss - 77, 92
Knapp, Jennifer - 121, 137

-L-
Led Zeppelin - 24, 75, 77, 125
Lennon, John - 42, 43, 46, 77, 120, 144
Lifehouse - 120-122
Lilith Fair Tour - 121, 136, 142
Luke 16:15 - 135

-M-
Madonna - 45, 130
Manson, Marilyn - 23, 86
Matthew 4:3 - 16
Matthew 5:21-22, 28 - 145

Matthew 7:16-20 – 128, 131
Matthew 13:19 – 16
Matthew 16:15-18 – 66
Matthew 16:23 – 17
McLachlan, Sara – 136, 137
Metallica – 34, 59, 69, 95, 102, 113
Morissette, Alanis – 77, 144
Motley Crue – 39, 47, 104
Mudvayne – 23

-N-
`N SYNC – 128, 138, 140, 141, 142
Naughty by Nature – 63
Numbers 32:23 – 98

-O-
Offspring – 108
Osbourne, Ozzy – 32-34, 50-56, 68-70, 81, 102, 144

-P-
Page, Jimmy – 24
Pearl Jam – 104
P.O.D. – 118, 119, 121, 122
Porno for Pyros – 80
Prince - chapter – 11, 12, 34
Proverbs 4:20 – 76
Proverbs 6:27 – 105
Proverbs 11:2 – 59
Proverbs 13:20 – 139
Proverbs 14:12 – 96
Proverbs 31:30 – 101
Proverbs 21:10 – 12
Psalms 40 – 87
Psalms 66:18 – 127
Psalms 149:1 – 117
1 Peter 5:8 – 16
2 Peter 2:1-19 – 138
2 Peter 2:19b – 65

-R-
Revelation 9:9,10,20 – 54
Revelation 12:9,10 – 16
Revelation 21:8 – 54, 55, 145
Revelation 22:15 – 54

Rolling Stones – 12, 27-31, 46, 56, 75, 83-84, 89, 104, 129
Romans 6:20-22 – 40
Run-DMC – 119

-S-
Santana – 78-80, 88, 144
Sixpence None the Richer – 121, 137
Skid Row – 77
Slayer – 86
Slipknot – 123, 124
Smashing Pumpkins – 104
Spears, Britney – 128-131, 138, 140-142
Sting – 24
1 Samuel 16:23 – 71

-T-
Titus 3:3 – 91
Townshend, Pete – 76
2 Live Crew – 133
2 Timothy 2:22 – 135
2 Timothy 2:26 – 52

-U-
U2 – 118, 121
Ugly Kid Joe – 90, 97

-V-
Van Halen – 32, 39, 136,

-W-
Who, The – 56, 76, 104

-Y-
Yoakam, Dwight – 110

ABOUT THE AUTHOR

Michael Bruce Plont graduated from high school and began a college-town music tour in hopes of "making it big" in a rock band. Along the way he received an associate's degree in criminal justice, and bachelor's degrees in Psychology, Political Science, and Law Enforcement – all before attending Messenger College.

While attending Messenger, Michael began to minister about the effects of popular music on his own life, the stronghold it caused and how the Lord Jesus set him free. Currently, Michael serves as Youth Pastor of MT. Zion Family Worship Center in Traverse City, Michigan. A popular speaker and Bible study teacher, Reverend Plont has spoken about popular music across the mid-west.

Plont is a native of Michigan. He and his wife, Kelli, reside in northwest lower Michigan with their two-year-old son.

To learn more about Michael Plont's ministry or to share a testimony or prayer request, please visit:

www.MichaelPlont.com